"Leonard Felder has combined the beauty and wisdom of Judaism with deep psychological insights and expertise to teach us how to bridge our differences—whether they be personal, political or religious—while retaining our dignity and convictions and still respecting each other. His combination of spiritual and creative techniques for making peace and accepting one another are exactly what we need in these divisive times. This is a book that everyone should read."

> **-Rabbi Susan Nanus**
> **Wilshire Boulevard Temple and Author of "If These Walls Could Talk," "Harvest of Fire," and "The Survivor"**

"'We See It So Differently' is a gift for all of us who are struggling to understand how to navigate this moment of incivility and political discord in American society. Felder brings together the wisdom of Jewish tradition and his many years of work with families and organizations in a powerful book that will help us find a way to rebuild both the public discourse and our interpersonal relationships that are so stressed and broken at this moment in time."

> **--Rabbi Mike Uram**
> **University of Pennsylvania Hillel and Author of "Next Generation Judaism"**

"In a time when our country is deeply divided, what could be more important than a book on how to talk to people whose views are different than our own—and maybe even learn something from the conversation. The Jewish teachings it explores are ancient, yet this book's usefulness is modern, compassionate and insightful."

> **--Lisa Loomer**
> **Award-winning playwright and screenwriter, "The Waiting Room," "Distracted," "Girl Interrupted," and "Two Things You Don't Talk About at Dinner"**

"'We See It So Differently' is a powerful reminder that relationships are built or destroyed depending on whether there is honest, kind and compassionate communication. In a world that is being consumed by divisive and hurtful speech, Felder's lessons are an important guide on how to dial it back—and lift it up."

--Craig Taubman
Singer/Songwriter, co-founder of "Friday Night Live
Shabbats" and "Jewels of Elul" Booklets

"'We See It So Differently' tackles one of the biggest problems of our time, the unwillingness to listen, the obstinacy of argument. Here's a most welcome spiritual guide for recognizing the tensions and working toward a solution."

--Marcia Milgrom Dodge
Tony-nominated director, choreographer, and faculty member, American Musical and Dramatic Academy

"In this book filled with Jewish wisdom, Leonard Felder explores issues which raise sparks (Israel, religion, politics, sexuality). Then he offers ways of disagreeing and discussing these heated topics without burning down our relationships and our shared Jewish concerns. When we disagree for the sake of heaven, good things can come. This valuable book shows how to make it happen."

--Janet Sternfeld Davis
Talmud Teacher and Coordinator of the Beit Midrash,
American Jewish University

"Len Felder's 'We See It So Differently' is a book for everyone. He takes nothing for granted, sees tough issues from a calm and balanced point of view, and goes step by step to approach problems which have made some of our friends, family members and groups into adversaries. As a family therapist myself, I endorse this book as a profound system for peace."

--Arva Rose
Licensed Family Therapist and co-founder of Jewish Women's Theatre

"This is a really important book that I'm glad I read because I deal with these dilemmas all the time with colleagues and congregants who have different points of view. I highly recommend you explore this book and take its remedies to heart."

--Rabbi Stan Levy
Co-founder Bet Tzedek Free Legal Services and Professor of Spiritual Development, Academy for Jewish Religion

WE SEE IT SO DIFFERENTLY

Creative Ways for Jews
to Make Peace
When Family Members
or Colleagues Disagree
About Religion, Politics,
and Other Issues

LEONARD FELDER, Ph.D.

Author of *The Ten Challenges* and
When Difficult Relatives Happen to Good People

Palmetto Publishing Group
Charleston, SC

We See It So Differently
Copyright © 2019 by Leonard Felder, PhD

First Edition

Printed in the United States of America

ISBN 13: 978-1-64111-554-4
eBook: 978-1-64111-555-1

Medical safety: Some of the topics in this book might bring up deep feelings. Each individual is unique and if you have been under the care of a physician or mental health professional, please follow what you and this person have agreed upon for your health and well-being.

Confidentiality: Some of the names and identifying details in the case examples found in this book have been changed to protect privacy and confidentiality.

DEDICATION

This book is dedicated to all the teachers, students, family members, and colleagues who listen with an open heart and a sense of mutual caring when someone has different ideas or experiences from your own ideas or experiences.

CONTENTS

Chapter One:

WHAT TO DO WHEN IT STARTS TO GET INTENSE

On a Sunday evening in late July in Detroit when I was 14, the humidity rose to such an unbearable level you could spot which of my extended family members were wearing antiperspirant (and which were unable to raise their hands and be sure).

On this particular night, more than 60 souls had squeezed into my immigrant grandparents' small two-bedroom home (with no air conditioning) on Freeland Street near Seven Mile Road in the northwest part of the Motor City.

The Fahrenheit got up to 97 degrees that day, but now at sunset it cooled to "only 92." I looked out the front window of my grandparents' living room and noticed that another 25 male relatives were gathered outside under the street lights along Freeland Street toward Pembroke Avenue listening to the Detroit Tigers baseball game on their car radios.

Suddenly one of the male relatives called out from the front door, "Time for a minyan."

I was the youngest person in the room. I had been asked to wear a white shirt with dark pants. A small, torn black ribbon had been pinned to my shirt pocket at the cemetery.

My mom had died 48 hours earlier after four exhausting years of cancer treatments. She was 46. The burial a few hours ago had been followed by platters full of deli food at my grandparents' home.

My grieving dad was a Holocaust survivor from Plauen, Germany who had lost most of his relatives in the camps and who didn't like to show emotion. My older sister felt deeply sad but she was trying to hold it together.

I was the younger kid and I had been up most nights the past seven months unable to calm my noisy brain and my pounding heart because I was terrified of losing my mom.

To my maternal grandfather and his religiously observant family members who were wedged into the living room for a chance to be part of the prayers that my grandfather's rabbi was about to lead, the word "minyan" meant at least ten men and definitely men only.

Suddenly I heard one of my much older cousins using a gruff voice to one of my elderly female cousins who was resting in a comfortable chair in the living room. "Go! You should go in the kitchen," he told her, "the minyan is about to start." He pointed with his index finger to make sure she took him seriously.

That elderly female cousin rolled her eyes in frustration, but then she stood up slowly and surrendered her comfortable chair to one of the middle-aged men streaming in the front door as the rabbi handed out small prayer books to the men.

I felt my face turning unusually warm and my heart started pounding. I thought about keeping my mouth shut, but then I flashed on a memory of my mother's gentle and caring face as she stood happily in front of the congregation a year earlier at my bar mitzvah with a tight, constricting lymphedema sleeve on her swollen right arm where her surgeries were still sorting themselves out in her fragile body. I thought, "Maybe I should say something for the women to be included."

Then I silently told myself, "Don't say anything. Don't make a scene."

But in the next moment, I heard my own voice shouting out loud, "This isn't right. Mom would have wanted the women to be in the living room. She would want the women to be part of the prayer service. This is wrong."

Several of the older men who were sardined into the corners of the packed living room looked at me with anger and disgust. One elderly cousin glared toward my father, as if to say, "You need to get this kid to shut up."

My grandfather looked at me with sadness in his eyes.

Immediately, my dad and my older sister grabbed me by my short-sleeved shirt and pulled me into my grandparents' dimly lit bedroom that smelled like numerous years of deep fried potato latke smoke as well as the lingering fragrances of several hundred Friday night boiled chicken, noodle kugel, and pickled cucumber dinners that all of us loved so much.

My father's face was bright crimson as he warned me, "Stop it right now! You're being ridiculous."

With tears in my eyes, I insisted, "No, I'm not being ridiculous. This shiva thing (the first week of mourning) is about Mom. She would want the women to be included. The women should stay in the living room."

My older sister said, "Dad's right. You're being ridiculous."

My father added, "This is your grandfather's house. Show some respect."

I felt numb. Confused. Agitated.

I eventually went back into the living room and watched in silence from the corner of the room as the men raced through the prayers.

A QUESTION FOR THE READER

Have you ever been in a situation somewhat like this, where someone you care about had a particular way of doing a religious event or an important life cycle moment so very differently from what you would have preferred…and it made you feel all bottled up inside?

Have you ever tried to shrug it off, but the frustration leaked out through your words, your tone of voice, or your facial expressions and it caused friction between you and this other person?

When you and the people around you are clashing about religion, politics, or other important issues, how do you stand up for what you believe without alienating those who see things differently? What's it been like in your own family, in your own workplace, or at the congregation where you are somewhat or very involved? Or in your marriage or when raising kids? How do you disagree without being disagreeable?

A LIFELONG QUEST FOR CREATIVE SOLUTIONS

I don't have all the answers. But I do have a lifetime of working as a licensed psychologist who has counseled several thousand families, numerous companies and non-profits, and dozens of congregations on how to prevent and resolve the conflicts that tend to arise around certain topics that seem to divide passionate people more than ever these days.

Topics such as:

- How do you talk about your personal beliefs or your most-cherished religious practices (or your discomfort with specific religious rules or political choices) without becoming adversarial with the person who sees it differently from how you see it?

- How do you talk about Israel (at family gatherings, at school, in your congregation, at your workplace, or at argumentative public forums) with someone who has a point of view that is painfully different from your own and somehow be able to stay on good terms and appreciate the merits of each of your clashing perspectives?

- How do you talk about election controversies, health care policy, economic fairness, immigration, LGBT issues, discrimination, environmental concerns, or other hot-button issues with someone who sees things very differently from how you see them?

- How do you talk about the details of planning a wedding, a bar or bat mitzvah, a celebration of a newborn, a holiday gathering, a funeral, a Shabbat gathering, or what to do about Jewish education for your children or grandchildren, without getting on each other's nerves or falling into a power struggle?

- How do you talk about your personal quest for meaning, purpose, healing, renewal, integrity, and sacredness in your life when you are talking with someone in your family or your workplace who has a very different belief system or a tendency to judge or minimize your feelings about these important topics?

A PERSONAL REALIZATION

When I was 14 at my grandfather's house, I didn't have much guidance on how to deal with my intense feelings. All I knew was that my heart was racing, and my thoughts were exploding.

But several years later I was taking a series of classes on Jewish spirituality and ethics from a wonderful teacher who guided us on the ideas suggested by the twelfth century physician, astronomer, theologian, and ethicist Maimonides (or Rambam, pronounced Rahm-bahm, which is an acronym for Rabbi Moses ben Maimon). Maimonides recommended three crucial steps to follow if you want to offer an opposing view to someone… and how to deliver it with love and decency, rather than blurt out some "in your face" comments with self-righteous anger or dismissive snarkiness.

If I had taken a class on the mindfulness methods of Maimonides prior to being faced with the upsetting situation of the men kicking the women out of the living room at the shiva gathering following my mother's death, I would have known how to:

MAKE SURE NOT TO PUBLICLY EMBARRASS SOMEONE. Maimonides and many other Jewish writers describe the importance of keeping in mind that the person you disagree with also has a precious soul, an easily wounded spirit, and a hidden spark of the Divine within him or her. Even if that person is loud, pushy, opinionated, or stubborn, the fact remains that he or she is still a vulnerable soul who gets hurt or even crushed by being criticized or contradicted in front of people.

There's a fascinating word in Hebrew that explores what happens when we act in a way that is cold, harsh, or dismissive toward someone with whom we disagree. The word is "Mahlbeen" and it has several meanings. On a physical level, it means to "make white" or "cause the blood to drain from the face." On a spiritual level, it means to crush someone's spirit or essence because you have treated them harshly with your words or your tone of voice. In terms of Jewish law and tradition, the Talmud says that "the person who makes someone else ashamed in the presence of others is as if this person has shed blood."

So when you or I are engaged in a heated conversation with someone, or a power struggle over whose way is going to prevail, how do we avoid "causing the blood to drain from the face" and how do we make sure not to crush the hidden spark of the Divine that is contained even in that family member or colleague who is so relentlessly opinionated?

In the Jewish mindfulness guidelines of Maimonides and many others, the first step is to breathe, remember this person in front of you has a holy spark of goodness and Divinity somewhere deep inside, and then make sure you talk with this person calmly and respectfully one-on-one where he or she will not be humiliated or embarrassed.

For example, if I had known these Jewish teachings when I was 14, I could have gently asked my beloved grandfather to have a short conversation in a side room where the two of us could hug, open up our hearts, admit that we are both in pain, and then brainstorm together on what options there might be for accommodating both what his traditional rules required and what several others in the family wanted for that shiva gathering.

Instead of confronting and embarrassing my grandfather in front of his rabbi and the many guests, I might have found him to be sufficiently caring and loving if I had taken him aside one-on-one and started by saying, "We both are in grief and we both want to do something holy to honor Mom's beautiful soul that is making its transition right now. You go first on what you would like and then I'll have a turn and then we'll see if there is a way that both of us can feel heard and included in whatever we come up with on possible ways to do this."

It's not easy to approach someone with whom you disagree and have an open heart and a willingness to listen respectfully. The adrenalin rushing through our bodies and the thoughts racing through our brains make it hard to do this mindfulness step and not just go off on the other person.

But if you breathe calmly for a moment and visualize the precious soul or the spark of the Divine that is hidden deep within this other human being, it can give you a shift in energy that allows you to approach this person with caring and teamwork rather than with harshness or self-righteous anger. I didn't know how to do this when I was 14, but after taking (and eventually teaching) many classes on Jewish methods for creating peace between clashing loved ones, I have seen how amazing these methods are for coming up with creative alternatives and win-win solutions.

MAKE SURE YOU AREN'T DUMPING ON SOMEONE ELSE FOR WHAT FIRST NEEDS TO BE ADDRESSED IN YOUR OWN CHARACTER OR PSYCHE. Here's a second step that can help enormously. Maimonides and other Jewish teachers had the brilliance to know that quite often we human beings blurt out at someone else for what we need to clean up in our own habits. In Jungian psychology it's called Shadow Work (examining and working on your own shadow self and hidden tendencies, rather than projecting them outward by accusing someone else). In Twelve Step programs, it's called, "Taking your own inventory rather than taking someone else's inventory."

In Jewish spirituality, we are urged each year at the High Holidays and each night before bedtime, to take a Heshbon, an accounting of where we tend to miss the mark and what we can do to grow closer to the kind of person we know we can be if we overcome some of our reactive habits and tendencies.

At the age of 14, I was quick to accuse my grandfather and my older relatives of being closed-minded and rigid. But in fact, I was not yet able to see that I probably had quite a strong tendency to be closed-minded and rigid myself. Like most people who feel passionate about their beliefs and preferences, I was sure on that night that my grandfather was 100% wrong and I was 100% right, and I had no willingness to hear another point of view from what I was certain was the correct point of view.

I didn't know yet the many insights from Jewish teachings that recommend examining one's own rigidity and self-righteousness rather than accusing others of being the ones who are rigid and self-righteous. In the biblical book of Zephaniah (one of the lesser-known of the 17 Jewish prophets you will find in the complete Hebrew Scriptures…some scholars suggest that Zephaniah was an Ethiopian Jew more than 2,700 years ago), it says, "Remove the chaff from yourself before attempting to remove it from others." In the Babylonian Hebrew Talmud from 2,000 years ago, Rabbi Nathan advised, "Reproach not your neighbor for a blemish that is yours."

In Jewish teachings, we are urged to get off our high horse and stop accusing others of what might be our own tendency or lingering habit. I wish I had known then that I was wasting valuable time and energy by wallowing in resentment for how the other relatives were acting.

What would have been far more productive and helpful in that intense moment at my grandfather's house is if I had looked at my own anger and said calmly to myself, "Lighten up a bit. These folks have every right to be asking to do things the way they are accustomed to doing things. You might need to understand their passion and their pain if you want to have a conversation about how to make sure your own passion and pain get taken seriously. Rather than using your energy to judge and condemn them, how about taking a breath and not being so judgmental and so condemning of anyone. We're in this together right now. We're all trying to find a way to express our grief."

Once again, it's not easy to do this. The self-righteous brain and the fiery emotions will tend to tip you in the direction of "I'm right and they're wrong. I'm pure and they're corrupt. I'm caring and they're insensitive."

You know the drill…you know how the brain works when we are feeling slighted or dissed.

But in Jewish spirituality, and in the often-repeated words of my beloved current teacher Rabbi Miriam Hamrell, whose weekly discussion group on Musar (Jewish teachings about working on one's character and daily interactions) that I have attended for the past 14 years, "If we point a finger at someone else, then we need to notice that at least three bent fingers are pointing back at ourselves. When things get heated, it's a good opportunity to look at one's own contribution to the tension and miscommunication, rather than pointing the finger or putting all the blame on others."

MAKE SURE TO COME UP WITH CREATIVE ALTERNATIVES THAT HONOR BOTH OF YOUR PERSPECTIVES AND BE WILLING TO GO FORWARD FOR THE SAKE OF PEACE AND HEALING RATHER THAN FOR THE SAKE OF YOUR EGO OR "SAVING FACE." Here's how this third suggestion can work. I imagine that if I had taken five or ten minutes in a side room to brainstorm calmly with my grandfather, we might have come up with several viable ways to remedy the tense situation. Possibly we could have agreed to do one traditional prayer minyan for the living room and an egalitarian male-and-female prayer minyan for the kitchen or the back yard (it certainly was warm enough that night and we wouldn't have needed jackets or sweaters).

Or we could have two different prayer services one after the other in the living room. Several of my aunts and female cousins could have led the second service. Or we could have had a feminist egalitarian male to lead the second service and make it creative and participatory so that those who didn't know Hebrew well could feel included.

Or we could have come up with the possibility that my grandfather and his rabbi truly needed the first night service to be traditional with no surprises, but that my grandfather would ask lovingly for all those who wanted to do something differently to set aside an evening later in the week for having a discussion or a creative prayer service that came from their hearts and their desire to elevate the soul of his daughter and my mom.

There were many possible ways to be inclusive of what he needed and what I needed. But first we had to get past the power struggle and the hurt feelings.

What I appreciate about Jewish spiritual methods for seeking peace when smart people disagree passionately is that they tend to be respectful and bridge-building for utilizing the best elements from many different points of view. We all know the joke that if you have ten Jews you have twenty opinions. But there's something holy and profound about a spiritual approach which says, "We are all created by the same creator. We are all parts of the whole. We all have some aspect of the wisdom of the world contained in our differing viewpoints. Now let's put the seemingly irreconcilable pieces together in a unique way that honors the One who created us all."

WHAT IS MEANT BY THE WORDS 'MAKING PEACE' IN THE SUBTITLE OF THIS BOOK?

Some people mistake the word peace or 'making peace' as meaning you will need to be docile, passive, shutting up to avoid conflict, or keeping things superficial and nicey-nice. But that's not what the word "Shalom" or "Making Peace" means.

Young children think of the word "Shalom" as meaning "hello" or "goodbye" or "peace." But as teens and adults we learn it also means "wholeness" or "completeness."

What Maimonides and many other Jewish scholars have taught us is that when we listen to a full diversity of viewpoints, then we get beyond the surface level and we can go deeper into the whole picture (including the subtle nuances and creative possibilities). It's like in the Talmud pages where you can see a full circle of diverse and clashing commentaries that draw out the possibilities and the depth of the phrase that is sitting in the middle of the page of text.

In Judaism it's not "I'm right and you're wrong," but rather that "you and I are in dialogue with each other and through our dialogue we both come to see innovative possibilities that we cannot see on our own, but only if we are willing to have a two-way brainstorming conversation." The person you exchange ideas with in a class or a study session is not called your "adversary," but rather your hevruta—your friend.

If you want to achieve peace between clashing viewpoints, we don't just talk in Judaism about passively "giving peace a chance," but rather we are urged to take specific actions to make sure we are "Rodef Shalom," a Hebrew phrase that means pursuing peace even when it's elusive or complicated. Peace is a journey of truly listening to each of the participants and working together to come up with solutions for which each individual can say, "Even if we didn't reach a 'perfect' outcome, at least each one of us does feel heard and included, so we can move forward together knowing that for now this is the most complete and whole outcome we've come up with thus far."

WHO CAN BENEFIT FROM THIS BOOK

A part of your brain might be saying, "Do I really need to have a conversation at all with the people who get on my nerves about religion or politics or Israel or other issues?" You might be asking, "Why can't I just write this person off and never deal with him or her again."

I understand the feeling. Believe me, I've got specific people in my own life whose preachiness or rigidity on certain issues can make your skin crawl.

But the fact remains that you and I live in a world where we have:

- Significant relatives we will see sooner or later at holidays, weddings, funerals, birthdays, and other events…and it would be great to have better tools for how to respond to the disagreements and power struggles that are likely to come up with this individual the next time you are both at the same event.

- Colleagues at work who get on our nerves because of their opinions regarding controversial issues and we need ways to defuse the tensions and still be able to work as teammates with this person on specific projects.

- Longtime regulars or occasional guests at the congregation or nonprofit organization you are involved with and these individuals tend to say things in a bossy or forceful way. Or they spout inflexible opinions about women's rights, LGBT issues, Israel, or other topics that make you want to cringe. Yet somehow we need to sit near this person at services or talk with this person at the buffet table or at meetings or group discussions. Wouldn't it be a relief to have some guidance on effective ways to restore the mutual respect and warmth you once had with this complicated individual?

Since this book is about Jewish mindfulness methods, I need to let you know that it doesn't matter if you are very religious, somewhat religious, barely religious, not at all religious, or not Jewish whatsoever in order to benefit from these ancient and modern teachings about resolving intense disagreements. Every type of Jew and every type of human being can become a much better listener, integrative problem-solver, and source for healing and repair as a result of exploring and utilizing these extremely-practical Jewish mindfulness methods for making peace and restoring decency to our heartfelt clashes of opinion.

Nor does it matter if you are politically conservative, moderate, liberal, progressive, radical, or "don't label me at all, thank you very much." This book is not about trying to convince anyone to agree 100% with anything. In fact, I urge you to feel free to disagree with anything you read in these six chapters and be willing to question or seek other opinions from people you know and trust.

Please try out these easy-to-utilize methods on your own and see which ones work immediately for you and the people in your life. Rather than biting your lip or pulling out your hair the next time you are around individuals who see things differently from you, imagine what it will feel like to be adept and successful at creating teamwork and warmth, rather than divisiveness and icy coldness. Our families, our workplaces, our congregations, and our world need us to start using these ancient and modern Jewish tools. Let's explore together what they are and why they are so highly effective.

Chapter Two:

HOW DO YOU FEEL ABOUT THE #MeToo ISSUES

Right now there are intense arguments flaring up in all sorts of places (families, companies, non-profits, schools, political races, churches, synagogues) about what constitutes sexual harassment or sexual misconduct. It's a topic that is causing people to take sides and get upset with one another. Not just about whether someone is guilty of crossing a line he or she shouldn't cross. But also about what to do in response.

Here is an example:

Several years ago, something strange happened in the waiting room of the suite of offices I was sharing at that time with eight other psychologists. I didn't see exactly what happened with my own eyes. But if I describe to you what the participants recall, you will be able to come to your own sense of what happened and how you feel about it.

Please put your seat belt on. It might be a bumpy ride (and I hope you will talk with a supportive friend or a trained counselor if this chapter brings up strong feelings or flashbacks from your own life experiences).

At five o'clock in the afternoon on a Wednesday, the small light on the wall in my office lit up and that means my five o'clock counseling client had arrived in the waiting room and had flipped up the switch that notifies me it's time to greet and escort the person into my office.

I walked down a short hallway and opened the door to the waiting area. That's where I saw my client, a highly-intelligent and creative Jewish woman in her 20's. She was in counseling primarily to talk about her sadness from losing her younger sister who died unexpectedly six months earlier at the age of 22.

In the waiting room, I could see my client looked somewhat upset about something. Her mouth and jaw seemed tight. Her eyes looked away and that was unusual for her because she usually makes very direct eye contact. Her brow was furrowed as if she was sorting out something complicated in her mind.

A minute later when we both sat down in my office, I offered her a cup of water and asked, "Is something upsetting going on?"

She was quiet for just a few seconds and then replied, "Who's the guy in the reddish hair with the Birkenstock shoes?"

I replied, "Was it one of the therapists from the suite?"

She shrugged her shoulders and explained, "I don't really know. He was short, intense, and kind of nerdy, like Woody Allen in the Annie Hall days."

I realized she was talking about a prominent therapist in the suite who was about five foot six, reddish-haired, Jewish, and in his 50's.

I said to my client, "That's one of the long-time therapists who originally remodeled the suite and rents out the offices to the rest of us."

My counseling client took a deep breath and then commented, "Well, he's got a bit of a problem. He came out to the waiting room to meet his client and he started staring at my chest. Not the one second stare that passes for o.k. these days. Or the three second stare that begins to get a little creepy. This was the twelve second stare that makes you feel like you want to run out of the room or go put on a loose-fitting hoodie jacket. Can you believe this guy thinks he's a therapist?"

I felt terrible and I think I said at that moment, "I am so sorry for what happened to you. That is not what's supposed to happen when you come to a counseling office."

In the next few seconds, I saw my counseling client become silent at first and then tears began to well up in her eyes. She reached for the box of tissues a few inches from her chair and then began to tell me about a number of times in her life when someone had stared at her for far too many seconds to the point of discomfort, as well as other times when someone she'd thought was trustworthy had tried to touch her inappropriately.

She then confided about a now-deceased male relative who had pressured her to do things she didn't want to do when she was a pre-teen and also when an especially handsome and charismatic former boyfriend wouldn't take no for an answer and she felt trapped in his car many miles from home.

As she told me, "I think of myself as a strong young woman but there have been several times in my life when I felt cornered or overpowered by someone. In the past, I usually would shut down or numb my feelings with food and gain a whole lot of weight after those situations. I don't want to do that this time. I don't want to let this creep shut me down or send me into a downward spiral."

THE BIGGER PICTURE

We are living in a time when the rules and norms of how to respect someone's body and private space are not what they were twenty or fifty years ago. It's not just the nationally televised moments of Professor Anita Hill confronting Supreme Court Justice nominee Clarence Thomas in 1991 or the recent hearings in 2018 on national television in which Professor Christine Blasey Ford confronted Supreme Court Justice nominee Brett Kavanaugh.

In the past five years, there have been hundreds of companies, churches, synagogues, and non-profit organizations where a top official or a key donor has been accused of being sexually aggressive, verbally inappropriate, or creating a hostile work environment. There are thousands of families where an uncle, a step-dad, a grandpa, a brother, or a father is being accused of crossing a line he should not have crossed in terms of emotional abuse, physical abuse, or sexual advances. There are also numerous women who have been accused of sexually harassing an employee, a student, or a family member, or who have been accused of being enablers of someone else's mistreatment of a vulnerable individual.

Whether in 2018 you believed Brett Kavanaugh or you believed Christine Blasey Ford is not what I will be discussing in this chapter. Rather, as a psychologist I will be exploring with you how you tend to feel about this rapidly changing aspect of our society and what are some healthy and creative ways to deal with these complicated situations and the clashing viewpoints they create.

So let me begin by asking you a few personal questions that you can answer silently, privately and honestly:

- Have you ever been in a situation where someone treated you in an inappropriate or uncomfortable way and you felt somewhat powerless to do much about it?

- Have you ever been the person who stared a little too long, said something flirty that made someone uncomfortable, pressured someone who was saying no, or caused someone to feel there was subtle favoritism going on in your family, at school, or at work?

- Have you ever felt unsure of whether to believe what someone was saying about an incident that you hadn't seen with your own eyes?

- Have you ever been in a situation where you or someone you know has been falsely accused by someone?

- Have you ever sensed that a charismatic person in a powerful position at school, at work, at a seminar or retreat, or in a congregation was giving extra attention or grooming someone to be his or her "special secret someone" and there was something unfair or exclusionary about the atmosphere from then on?

THE ARGUMENTS AND TENSIONS THAT LINGER

When someone does something that goes too far and makes another person feel uncomfortable at work, at school, or at a social event, all sorts of problems tend to happen. For example:

- If someone at work or school is being sexually invasive or inappropriate with words or touching directed toward a co-worker, student, customer or associate, nearly everyone in the organization gets caught up in the gossip, the rumors, and the uncertainty of who to believe and who not to believe. Every day people come to work not knowing if today's the day that you will be asked to choose a side or to get questioned on what you know and when you knew it. Or whether the powerful person being accused is going to be fired or possibly given a raise and allowed to continue in power (and possibly seek revenge on those who doubted his or her innocence).

- When someone in your extended family is accused of being sexually aggressive or inappropriate with words or touching, it's likely to cause all sorts of havoc each time the family tries to get together for a holiday, a birthday, or a life cycle event. Do you really feel o.k. sitting next to Uncle Awkward when you have been told that this person has been accused of something? But what if you love this person a lot and you have doubts about whether the accusations are true? How do you walk the tightrope of honoring the humanity of the accuser and honoring the humanity of the accused?

- When a public figure or a famous person gets accused, you will often find that people start having arguments with each other about whether to believe the allegations and what to do about the beloved public figure who has been accused. I remember in 2018 when Charlie Rose the charming interviewer on television got accused of sexual misconduct, one of my counseling clients was upset about his leaving The CBS Morning Show and she said to me during a therapy session, "My best friend and I have been arguing about this for several weeks. My friend says Charlie Rose has got to go--end of discussion. I say I don't care what Charlie Rose does in private. I miss him, his soothing voice, his way with words, and I want him back on my television as soon as possible. As a result, my best friend and I are both feeling a little bit estranged from each other."

Another one of my therapy clients was upset about a major donor and board member for an important charity who was accused of sexual misconduct in 2019 and it caused donations to drop considerably for that particular charity. My client commented, "Why does a good organization dedicated to helping people have to lose out because one of the major donors and board members is a sleaze? Why can't we handle these things in private and keep our mouths shut like in the old days." This client and several of her friends had been arguing for weeks about whether to stop contributing to that charity. They also disagreed with each other about whether it was "idle gossip" to talk about the donor's scandal or whether it was "necessary important disclosures to prevent future incidents."

THE SADNESS AND THE DISAGREEMENTS

A sexual misconduct incident might take only a few seconds to happen, yet it can have implications and after-effects that last for many years or even decades. For instance, take a moment to consider the intense ongoing debate and passionate disagreements that arose about Senator Al Franken and what happened when he was accused of sexual misconduct.

I had always enjoyed Al Franken as a down-to-earth Midwestern Jew who had gone to Harvard and was quite funny and brilliant. Like most Americans, I first had some good laughs from his sketch writing and his performances on Saturday Night Live, where he seemed like a vulnerable dorky guy with a big heart. Then I listened to his political/comedy radio show every morning on the way to work during 2004-2007, where each day he cracked me up with his humorous discussions of various corrupt or extremist characters in the political world. I also loved that he was so open about how much he adored his wife Franni and their two children.

Then a few years later when he became a Senator from Minnesota, he grew into a well-respected leader on many important causes and crucial pieces of legislation. He eventually became a key member of the powerful Senate Judiciary Committee, asking probing questions of judicial appointees and busting the chops of various government officials who were corrupt or dishonest.

Like many people, I was sad and surprised in 2017 when Senator Franken was accused of several incidents of inappropriate behavior. There were photos of his putting his hands over the breasts of a fellow entertainer who was asleep on a USO tour. He was accused of forcing an excessive unwanted kiss more than once on a woman in a skit they were doing. More than one woman recalled his hands going where they should not be (and lingering for five or ten seconds) when she was posing with him for a photograph. One of his aides reported that he attempted to force a kiss on her and when she refused his advances he allegedly said, "It's my right as an entertainer."

Some of my colleagues and friends in 2017 wanted Senator Franken to resign immediately and have some privacy away from the media glare to work on his personal issues. They also felt they didn't want him to be the most visible person on the very important Senate Judiciary Committee who would be investigating the indiscretions of others. As one of my friends commented, "How the heck is Al Franken going to have any credibility to confront Attorney General Jefferson Sessions who says, 'I don't recall that meeting with the Russians…' if Franken is the guy who says, 'I don't recall that meeting with the woman whose breast I touched for ten seconds.'"

On the other hand, when Al Franken quickly got pressured to resign from the Senate, several of my friends and colleagues were furious (and are still furious) that Franken did not have a chance for a full hearing or full due process from the Ethics Committee of the Senate. One of my work colleagues thought it was unfair that Franken's attempts at an apology were quickly ignored and considered "not enough."

Numerous people I know are still viscerally angry at Senator Kirsten Gillibrand of New York who led the efforts to urge Franken to resign from the Senate. According to one of my female friends, a college professor who is a strong advocate for women's issues but who feels Franken was not given due process, "In light of what President Grab-Em has said and done, I will never understand why there was such a rush to judgment against Al Franken by Senator Gillibrand."

As with many sexual misconduct situations, the allegations against him had stirred a lot of people up and the anger and resentments in both directions weren't dying down even after some time passed.

More than a year after Franken had exited from public life, there were long articles in The New York Times and in The Atlantic quoting numerous prominent individuals who were still extremely upset about how Al Franken was rushed out of Washington. There were also news reports that said major donors to the 2020 Presidential candidates had told each other to stay away from donating to Senator Gillibrand because they could not forgive her for how harsh she was in her statements about Al Franken.

Senator Gillibrand was asked by an interviewer on national television in March 2019 why she had angered so many people by being one of the first to speak out against Senator Al Franken. Gillibrand took a deep breath and replied:

"In terms of Senator Franken, this is a very hard issue for so many Democrats because we miss him and we loved him. But he had eight credible allegations against him of sexual harassment for groping, two of them when he was a Senator, and the eighth one that came out was a congressional staffer.

"I had to make my choice of whether to be silent or not. I am a mother of boys and the conversations I was having at home were very upsetting because Theo (her son) said to me, 'Mom! Why are you so tough with Al Franken?' And as a mother I had to be really clear. It's not o.k. for anyone to grope a woman anywhere on her body without her consent and it is not o.k. to forcibly kiss a woman ever without her consent. It was not o.k. for Senator Franken and it is not o.k. for you Theo. Ever!

"So I had to be clear. And if there are some powerful donors who are angry because I stood up for women who came forward with accusations of sexual harassment, that's on them."

If you are part of a school, a company, a non-profit, a congregation, or a family where there has been an accusation of sexual misconduct, how do you prevent or resolve the feuding and grudge-building that can tear apart some or all of the important credibility you have spent years establishing together? How do you make sure a sexual misconduct moment doesn't drive a wedge between people who need to work together, celebrate together, pray together, or learn together? Is there something each of us can do to recover from these controversies and to respect the humanity of the accusers and also respect the humanity of the accused?

WHAT JEWISH MINDFULNESS TEACHINGS CAN OFFER

There are some gems of wisdom from Jewish teachings that can help in situations where you and the people around you are arguing, taking up sides, or trying to decide what to do about these complicated sexual incidents. I've found these profound and practical Jewish teachings extremely helpful for giving me guidance on how to sort out the issues and respond in a way that re-establishes peaceful, healthy teamwork during and after a controversial allegation has occurred, even if people have somewhat different viewpoints of how to interpret the facts.

Whether you have an extensive background in Jewish teachings, or a little bit of background, or even if you are not very interested in Jewish teachings for the most part, see if these ancient and modern Jewish insights can help you navigate the stormy seas of sexual misconduct accusations and denials:

TAKE A MOMENT TO NOTICE IF YOU HAVE FAVORITISM AND THEN MAKE SURE TO SEEK IMPARTIALITY AND FAIRNESS. For thousands of years, Jewish writings have shined a light on how easy it is for even the smartest humans to become biased, swayed by certain factors, or fooled by a situation without fully sticking to the facts. The human brain and the human emotions can readily get caught up in the charisma of the accused, the status or lack of status of the accuser, or the "sophisticated" arguments that may or not be factually correct. (I remember as an undergraduate at Kenyon College how my jaw dropped when I found out from a Classics professor that the word "sophisticated" comes from the same Latin word as "sophistry," which means to use elegant language to deceive someone or "make the weaker argument the stronger one by the deceptive nature of the speaker's artistry").

For more than 3,000 years Jewish teachings have said, "Watch out for the tendency to give favor to someone who is actually not telling the full truth and be careful that your personal feelings don't cause you to stop listening to the one who is being 100% truthful."

Here is a quick version of how the Jewish passion for fairness and impartiality became such an important part of how we deal with complicated situations like the #MeToo accusations we are discussing in this chapter:

In the Book of Exodus, mostly in Chapter 19, Moses seems to be getting overwhelmed at trying to lead a huge community of several hundred thousand Hebrews traveling through the harsh desert. Moses desperately wanted to be fair each time one of them came up to him and accused someone else of a crime or a personal affront, but on any given day, so many people were lining up to bring Moses their personal disputes, it was exhausting. Moses was being asked to intervene in such a large number of squabbles and dilemmas that he didn't have time to investigate the facts or dig too deeply into the complicated issues.

On an especially overloaded day when Moses was feeling burned out and frustrated at the intensity of the disputes he was being asked to mediate, Moses spoke with his father-in-law Yitro who said, essentially, "Don't give yourself a hernia trying to figure out so many complicated situations each week on your own. Instead, put together a group of trustworthy judges and small group leaders who are not corrupt or self-serving. Ask God for guidance and teach all of these judges and sub-group leaders the principles of settling disputes fairly so that the community won't splinter into clashing sides and instead they can reach the longed-for destination with a lot less turmoil and distress."

Moses took to heart what Yitro had recommended and then Moses got quiet and listened to the voice of Divine wisdom that spoke to him from deep inside. This inner voice of Wisdom warned Moses that favoritism and unfairness will tear the community apart and that each judge and each decision-maker has to be extremely careful not to favor either the rich person or the poor person, and not to favor the person you feel biased toward or biased against.

In several different chapters, the Torah then explains in detail how important it is to have witnesses, factual evidence, cross-examination, caution in convicting someone, multiple points of view from a panel of decision-makers, and the careful monitoring of judges and sub-group leaders to make sure they don't get swayed by partiality but are able to stick to the facts and the evidence.

These chapters from the Torah reveal a remarkable breakthrough in human history. Even though the Exodus story took place at a time more than 3,500 years ago when most societies let the powerful kings, the enormously wealthy, or the most physically aggressive have their way in settling disputes, Jewish teachings broke the mold and said instead:

"You shall not be partial in judgment. You shall hear the small and the great alike." (Deuteronomy 1:17)

"You shall not be partial to the poor or defer to the great, but in righteousness shall you judge." (Leviticus 19:15)

If you use these core teachings in deciding what to do about an incident or an allegation, it helps you remember to look carefully and honestly to uncover your own biases and try harder to look at the facts, the evidence, the witness corroborations, and to hear the testimony of the accuser and the accused with a search for truth rather than a pre-existing partiality that causes a premature conclusion. I'll admit these ancient teachings are just as difficult and crucial to adhere to today as they were 3,500 years ago because we can so easily be swayed by our biases and our sense of favoritism. Can we truly listen and can we truly be fair to one another as we journey together during times of conflict?

In addition, numerous Jewish teachings many centuries after the Exodus story also look at how complicated it is for us as individuals to be impartial and to genuinely seek the facts and the fairness that are so important to prevent a community, a family, a workplace, a school, or a non-profit organization from descending into factions, friction, and divisiveness.

For example, in the Talmud and the Mishnah (the commentaries and discussions of the Torah laws as they applied to later centuries), there are some fascinating illustrations of how we humans feel conflicted in our guts and our minds when someone we admire is accused of doing something inappropriate that has consequences for the entire group or community.

One of the most useful illustrations of what to do when you feel conflicted or are arguing with someone about an allegation that is driving a wedge between people can be found in a short passage from the Mishnah "Mo-ed Qatan" (17a) in which one of the revered teachers in the community is being accused of some inappropriate behaviors.

Someone asked Rabbi Yehuda which way we should lean on the question of whether to denounce and remove this possibly offending teacher or whether to side with him or keep silent.

Rabbi Yehuda thought deeply on the issue and offered an insightful response, saying essentially, "We need him desperately as a teacher and we can't afford to lose him. But on the other hand, what he is doing is causing God's name to be profaned, so we need to examine the allegations carefully and possibly to stop him or remove him if the evidence is genuine."

In other words, the integrity and credibility of a community or a small group depends on being impartial and standing up to even the most revered person if that person is dragging the community through the dirt or if that person is disrespecting the preciousness of God's creations.

Rather than letting a sexual misconduct allegation cause people to take sides and hold grudges against one another, the Jewish teachings say we need to be working together as genuine teammates for seeking truth and listening to the wisdom of both sides (those who say, "Make sure the accused gets a fair hearing" and those who say, "Make sure the accuser gets a fair hearing.") Instead of fighting with each other as to which side is more correct, the Jewish approach is to say, "Appreciate that both of these points of view are what makes the process fair. Respecting the accuser and respecting the accused creates the balance and fairness that can keep a community or a family thriving, because if we lose that sense of balance and fairness it can tear the community or family apart for a long, long time."

REACH OUT TO SUPPORT PEOPLE FOR SEEKING GENUINE HEALING AND REPAIR. Here's a second way that Jewish teachings are different from what usually goes on during and after an allegation of sexual misconduct.

Usually the media, the rumors, and the gossip tend to focus on the fact that someone got accused of something scandalous and whether that person will lose his or her job, income, reputation, or other forms of punishment or public shaming. It becomes a game of "gotcha" where the emphasis is on chasing down and exposing someone so that they can be shunned from the community or the group. Then after the public exposure and the trial are over, the person is no longer in the news and is rarely discussed or cared about.

In Jewish history for thousands of years, there has been a somewhat different approach that focuses not only on holding a fair and impartial trial, but also on the steps toward repair and healing. For example, when a Jewish individual says or does something inappropriate, the community not only doesn't push this person away permanently but we actually become actively involved with this person as someone who needs the community's support and resources to find genuine healing and repair. We also become actively involved with the person who made the accusation to make sure that she or he gets the support, the counseling, the caring, and the creative next steps forward to heal and repair (to the extent possible) whatever was harmed or wounded by the incident in question.

In Judaism there's a strong effort made to help and respect any vulnerable soul who wants to do "teshuvah," a word that means to change or move toward a better direction, a holy direction, or a healing direction.

Teshuvah has several steps: to be honest about what caused someone discomfort, to feel genuine remorse, to make amends for when we missed the mark previously, and to get help to make sure the next time we can avoid hurting or harming anyone (including ourselves).

The accused person can choose to begin a sincere process of teshuvah (for turning his or her life toward healing and repair) after a controversial incident. The accuser and the bystanders also can choose to begin a sincere process of teshuvah (or healing and repair) because of how the incident caused so much discomfort, pain, and loss of direction in their lives as well.

In Jewish mystical teachings, the broken parts of ourselves and our communities are not to be discarded or ignored, but rather to be explored as a way toward profound healing. Quite often we hear people quote the singer/songwriter Leonard Cohen as saying, "There's a crack in everything, that's how the light gets in." (In fact, Cohen was quoting some of his Jewish relatives and teachers in Montreal and Los Angeles who were students of Jewish mysticism, which has several beautiful descriptions of how glimmers of light can emerge from the broken parts of who we are).

Both traditional and modern Judaism teach that there is a type of deep healing and renewal which can only occur when we examine and work on our own brokenness. In the Talmud (Berachot 34b) it says, "There is an honored place where an individual who is transforming a personal failing can stand and where a thoroughly righteous individual is not entitled to stand."

Rather than looking down at someone who has gotten twisted up in a sexual misconduct situation, we are taught in Judaism to look at this individual as an honored soul who might possibly be on a journey of healing and repair that is worthwhile and in need of support. Instead of turning your back on this person, it makes you want to engage with this person and be of service.

Here are two quick examples of how to follow through on the Jewish teachings to be of service to someone who has been the accuser or the accused in an incident of sexual misconduct. I hope these true stories will inspire you to reach out and be a source of support and healing for someone in your own life who has been impacted by a complicated situation involving sexual misconduct or a hostile work environment:

The first example is a woman who told me in a counseling session that many years ago when she was a teenager in a Jewish youth group she was treated as "special" by her very handsome and charismatic male cantor. The cantor helped teach her to play the guitar and engaged in long talks about important topics with her. This woman recalled being 16 and "feeling like young Courtney Cox in the t-shirt and jeans during the Bruce Springsteen video of 'Dancing in the Dark,' where the singer spots her looking up at him in the crowd below, calls her up on the stage, and dances with her one-on-one in front of everyone. She feels so chosen, so special, so fortunate."

The guitar lessons and the special treatment also included a lot of hugs that went a little too long, some kisses that became a little too passionate, some shoulder and back rubs partially clothed, and a sense that 'None of the boys my age meant much to me because I had this sizzling attention from this very powerful figure who everyone thought was so amazing.'"

Years later this woman had gotten divorced from her husband and came for counseling to try to understand why she had never quite felt for her husband what she had felt for the cantor. We discussed in therapy that one of the rarely-explored aspects of being sexually groomed by a powerful adult as his "special secret someone" included a confusion that many molestation survivors experience, namely that the sizzle of being "chosen as special and unique by the person in power" can cause a lifelong challenge of not quite being able to form a peer-to-peer bond or feel the same sizzle with a more appropriate romantic partner of your own age or social status.

As this woman described to me in counseling, "I had no idea that the turn-on I felt being picked as special by this cantor would linger and become an obstacle that has impacted each of my adult relationships."

During one of our counseling sessions, she sat up straight in her chair with a sense of strong determination and said, "I need to reclaim my own sensuality and worth, rather than continue to be under the spell of this manipulative adult who had his own issues and who didn't stop to think how his flirtations would affect my life and my ability to relate to a peer. I need to break free of the grip he's had on me for far too long."

As part of our counseling, we did two things to help this woman get back what had been taken from her by the emotionally-confusing experience from her youth group days. First, we decided to locate the cantor and explore with him in a carefully refereed therapy session what this woman had never been able to tell him previously and to help him understand how his seductive actions had impacted this woman's personal life. That powerful counseling session and confrontation resulted in the cantor truly listening to her hesitant feelings for the first time and apologizing to her for the unintended harm he had caused.

The second thing we did was to find a local sexual abuse and molestation survivors' organization that this woman joined first as a participant and later as a speaker, an advisor, a fundraiser, and a board member. As this counseling client explained to me during the final session when we wrapped up the excellent work she had done, "I needed to hear the experiences of other young women who were smart and strong but got misled by an adult who was a lot more savvy about how to groom someone and get sexual favors from them. I needed to explore with other survivors how to regain the sense of joy, honesty, and sensuality I had hidden away after that confusing experience when I was 16. I'm finding now that I do have the ability to experience sizzle and safety again in my personal life after years of feeling numb and disconnected. It's sad how many years I was adrift because of what I experienced when I was a teenager."

If you or someone you know has been impacted by sexual misconduct, there are many ways to turn this lingering pain or confusion into healing. The Jewish journey of teshuvah or turning in a holy direction might include not only to explore and repair what was injured in one person's life but also to offer support and healing steps to others who are on a similar journey. Please reach out and find the empowering counselors, groups or organizations where you can turn what was once broken and do the important work to make sure this painful chapter of one's life becomes a source of renewed light, strength, and health.

The second example is a man I knew for many years when we were active staff members at a summer workshop in the San Bernardino Mountains of Southern California called "Brotherhood/Sisterhood USA" which was sponsored by the National Conference of Christians and Jews. Each summer during a week of seven 12-hour days there was a multi-racial, religiously-diverse staff who volunteered to help 200 high school students from the Los Angeles area (everyone from East LA gang members to middle class immigrant teens from Glendale and Long Beach to rich private school kids from Beverly Hills, Santa Monica and Woodland Hills) to get to know each other and discuss the issues of racism, sexism, homophobia and religious prejudice at a very intense human relations dialogue of equals that opened many eyes and won lots of awards.

What I didn't know during those first eight years as a volunteer staff member is that my friend who was the co-director of the workshop was not just the articulate, compassionate, wise role model he seemed to be to all of us at the summer workshops. We discovered one summer that he was being accused of grooming one student every few years at the high school where he was an award-winning teacher to be his "special friend" and he had been having secret affairs for more than a decade. This was a shock not only to his wife, his kids, and all of us who loved him dearly, but also to the staff and campers that only knew him as a powerful male figure and role model at the workshops.

For the first two years after the allegations exposed a history of secrets, deceptions, and cover-ups, there were warring factions within the organization. Most people sided with the wife of the accused teacher and they vowed never to speak to him again. A few tried to defend his actions as being "the product of a different era when he came of age in which the rules were not so strict." Still others were upset with the organization for not taking action quickly enough and for letting this teacher continue in his role as a leader and role model for almost a year while the rumors and disclosures were being handled in private conversations. It was a sad mess and many people got hurt by the chaos that erupted.

After he got suspended as a teacher and ordered by a court to join a perpetrator's group, I was in a conversation with several of the summer workshop's long-time staff who were mostly in agreement that none of us should have anything to do with this individual any longer. I understood their position and I didn't quite agree.

I wanted to understand what caused this award-winning teacher to mess up and what could be done to repair the chaos that resulted from his affairs. So I began to meet informally one-on-one with this banished individual and it grew into a few hours a month for several years. It wasn't therapy. Nor was it taking sides. It was just two souls taking walks together, having lunch conversations together, and having follow-up phone calls to listen to one another and see what kind of healing and repair might be possible.

We were honest with each other. He told me how ashamed he felt and how he had let down his family, his friends, and his profession. He told me how angry and hurt he was at how judgmental and dismissive so many people were with him.

He told me that he had felt at first that the perpetrator's group was below him in terms of education level and status in life, but that he had come to understand how he truly was similar to most of the men in the group at having been sneaky and controlling about sexuality from a very early age. With tears in his eyes, he admitted at one of our lunches, "I feel like I've been a controlling and manipulative sneak my entire life. I wish there were some way to repair the damage I've caused and to be able to start over somewhere."

I told him my honest truth as well. On one visit when I saw that he was severely depressed, I let him know that I was worried he might kill himself and yet I was hopeful that he would someday be able to turn this into something healing and helpful. It wasn't all politeness between us-- I also made sure to gently say something each time I thought he was being dishonest or evasive. As he admitted to me during one of our walks, "You need to bust me whenever you think I'm lying to myself or to you. I have a long history of being sneaky. I need to be confronted or else I'll slip back into those old habits."

Several times when we talked, there were uncomfortable moments where he accused me of being judgmental and I had to look deep inside to see if he was accurate or not. I admitted to him a few times when he was correct about my being somewhat judgmental and I did my best to listen again with an open heart. I also told him truthfully several times that he seemed to be making progress during the four years he was doing some profound soul searching with his personal counselor at the perpetrators' group that he attended consistently.

I am happy to report that as a result of this complicated individual doing several years in his perpetrator's group and making amends to each of his family members, to many of the workshop staff, and to four of his former students, some teshuvah and healing did take place. Specifically, he is not allowed to teach or work with people under 21, but he has found numerous other ways to be an advocate for the homeless, the mentally ill, and those who have been in prison and are now looking for jobs and respect. He has established a healthy relationship of equals with a woman his age who appreciates how hard he has worked on his personal issues.

He lives in another state now and I still talk on the phone with him every few months. For me he is a warning red light that flashes and says, "Don't manipulate someone and delude yourself into thinking it's ok." He's also a real-life example that says to me and others who know him today that, "Even someone who falls very far in a downward direction can do the hard work of teshuvah to become a renewed source of healing and wholeness once again."

If there is someone in your life who has fallen severely because of his or her sexual urges or lack of healthy boundaries, I hope you will consider finding a way to connect with this person's soul and assist this person if he or she is willing to do the sincere steps and efforts to heal what has been broken. As I see it, we can either judge and shun the people who struggle in life, or we can support them in turning their gifts in a more holy and positive direction. You get to decide.

BE AWARE THAT ALMOST EVERY PERSON NEEDS SOME PREVENTIVE TOOLS FOR WHEN THEIR IMPULSES ARE SIMMERING AND TROUBLE COULD HAPPEN. The third and final Jewish teaching on how to deal with sexual misconduct is all about prevention. For thousands of years, Jewish scholars and teachers have explored with their students and colleagues the fact that we all have a strong creative life force inside of us that can help us to do amazing positive things or that same strong creative life force can cause us to do some hurtful, insensitive, or dishonest things as well.

I've always been impressed at how realistic and practical Jewish teachings have been on this subject. For a moment, consider these three insights about mindfulness and prevention that come from Jewish sources many centuries ago:

- Rabbi Isaac two thousand years ago suggested that "Sexual thoughts are so hard to stop that even during the time when a man is in mourning his impulse is apt to give him trouble."

- The founder of the Hasidic movement almost four hundred years ago, the Baal Shem Tov, was asked if there is a way a person could discern a true religious leader from a false one. The Baal Shem Tov answered, "Ask him if he knows a way to prevent lustful thoughts. If he says he does, he is a charlatan."

- The Baal Shem Tov also is reported to have offered another way of coping mindfully with the lustful and sexually curious thoughts that can distract your mind or cause you to do something inappropriate that might create havoc for a person, an organization, a congregation, or for the integrity of your holy work. It is reported that the founder of Hasidism told his followers that instead of feeling overwhelmed and guilt-ridden for having a brief lustful thought, it is much more effective to appreciate the God-given beauty of that individual by refocusing your thoughts back on the Creator and the awesomeness of all of God's creations. You then have the ability to elevate your active brain from focusing on lust or sneakiness and shift your thoughts instead to a renewed appreciation for the holiness of all things.

> In other words, in Judaism the goal is to consciously manage and re-direct the urge to stare, the urge to say something provocative that might cause discomfort, or

the urge to do something you know deep in your heart is not what you were put on this earth to do. There is a sense of humbleness and vulnerability about these teachings. Scholars and advisors throughout Jewish history have come right out and said essentially, "Be careful with your susceptible human soul because you are definitely going to have moments of being tempted. If your eyes or your thoughts have a moment when they begin to stray, you are likely to start trying to rationalize or justify your hurtful desires. You better have a plan on what you are going to do at the exact moment when the urge to be sneaky, manipulative, or sexually inappropriate flares up. Otherwise you will slip sideways into something complicated with huge consequences for yourself, your loved ones, your community, and some vulnerable people who thought they could trust you."

Rather than pretending these urges aren't going to challenge you every so often, the Jewish approach is to be alert to the early warning signs that your eyes, your words, or your imagination are starting to drift into places you don't want to be going. In Judaism, the primary word for sin (khatah or missing the mark) has an archery metaphor in which we mindfully notice we are aiming the quiver and the arrow a little bit off center and we gently re-direct our aim toward the higher or more appropriate target.

As an example of how prevention and pro-active re-directing works in a Jewish context, please take a moment and consider what many Jewish leaders and professionals have begun doing recently to deal much more effectively with their own inner urges:

A few years ago, I was asked to lead a weekend workshop for 250 rabbis, cantors, Jewish pastoral counselors, and congregational staff members on "Jewish Methods for Dealing with Sexual Feelings Toward Students, Congregants, and Others." It was a very honest and emotionally-intense weekend because nearly all of these individuals were willing to deeply examine their own struggles with sexuality, favoritism, and the unspoken confusion that happens when there is an unintended sexual chemistry with a student, a congregant, a colleague, or someone else besides one's primary partner.

As a result of listening to these 250 individuals and thousands of other men and women over the years, I've found there are some fascinating reasons why nearly every person in a position of power or influence tends to have at least a few moments of being tempted to do something that might step over the line toward sexual misconduct or seductive favoritism. Here are a few you can think about as you examine your own temptations in this area or the temptations you have witnessed in others:

- I've found that the vast majority of adult professionals in all sorts of fields have at least one moment when they are attracted to someone other than their primary partner and there is a subconscious feeling of "Wow, I'm now in a position of respect or power such that this attractive or dynamic person is drawn to me in ways that I could never have experienced when I was a gawky teenager. It feels intoxicating that someone as attractive as this person who wouldn't have given me the time of day when I was an insecure young person is now looking up to me. Flirting with this person makes me feel like I've finally arrived and I'm no longer the awkward, insecure person I was all those years ago."

Saying no to that persistent urge to flirt with or to give a lot of extra attention to that attractive or admiring student, congregant, or colleague is not easy. Many men and women in positions of power rush into a flirtation or a seduction of the student, congregant, colleague or other attractive individual instead of remembering, "This is probably not what a responsible sane person in a position of power or influence is here to do—courting and seducing someone who is not my primary partner. This is probably going to be a mess if I don't re-direct my energies quickly. How about if I enjoy the fact that this person finds me worthy or attractive, but not to act goofy or manipulative and ruin a holy moment with something sneaky or irreversible that is going to end up hurting a lot of innocent people."

• I've also found that the vast majority of adult professionals in most fields and careers have a deep desire to be admired, appreciated, respected, or loved. There's nothing wrong with that. But if you let that insistent desire or urge for appreciation slip into something sexual, flirtatious, secretive, or manipulative, it usually stops being a harmless sense of being respected and starts being a frantic addiction of "I hope I don't get caught" and "I hope I can cover up all the clues and evidence that would cause people to suspect I've stepped over the line with someone."

Knowing ahead of time if you have an intense inner longing to be admired and appreciated means that you can then choose mindfully and carefully how to make sure that very-human longing doesn't cause you to favor one verbally admiring or highly-attractive student over another student who has the guts and honesty to be skeptical of some of your ideas. Knowing and admitting to yourself or a counselor that you have a deep longing to be loved and respected gives you a chance to ask yourself cautiously, "Is my urge to be special and unique causing me to disregard or cut short the diverse students, colleagues, congregants, clients, and friends who aren't lavishing me with affection. Am I treating someone like chopped liver and in fact that person has a soul and a life path that needs to be honored as much as those who are much more flattering, deferential, and loyal to me."

- Finally, I've found that many people think they have a right to stare a little too long, hug a little too sensually, say a few things that are somewhat inappropriate, or have a secretive affair because they feel, "It's owed to me after all I've had to endure." I've heard many highly-educated and highly-successful people say to me, "I just think that if you work your butt off to get to a position of authority and you can get away with something, it's not the end of the world to break the rules sometimes." Or they say, "Life isn't always fair or nice. If someone gets stared at, touched, or talked to in a way that makes them uncomfortable, they need to toughen up."

> For many individuals in earlier generations, that sense of entitlement or "getting away with it" did not have the same severe consequences for most individuals thirty or fifty years ago that they have today. All sorts of supervisors were chasing all sorts of employees around the desk and getting away with it "back in the day."

> But it's probably time to say hello to the new world. Right now if you cross that line, you are at risk of losing everything you have built in both your career and your private life. Knowing ahead of time that there will be severe consequences means asking yourself, "Am I in

control here, or are my urges calling the shots. Am I really willing to risk everything for a few moments of trying to get away with something I know is not healthy for me or for the organization I've spent so many years trying to build up."

As a psychologist who has listened to many anxious individuals who had been "found out" after a sexual indiscretion, I've come to believe that the crucial first step in preventing a messy situation from happening is to face one's own insecurities and urges, rather than acting them out on someone else. Instead of letting your barely-conscious urges cause you to put your career, your credibility, or your loved ones in jeopardy, this allows you to take a breath, ask God or your inner wisdom for strength, and say no to the habit of giving too much sexual gamesmanship to a moment that needs to stay professional and appropriate.

It's not easy to do, especially if you are extra hungry sometimes for affection, admiration, or a loving touch. But in the words of one of my counseling clients, "I used to think I was nothing but a bunch of impulses and drives. Now I realize I've also got the ability to listen to the voice of compassion and the voice of deeper purpose that I've been exploring with various spiritual readings and classes as I've started to mature. I've come to realize I have the ability to do the reasonable thing, even in situations where my adrenalin and my impulses are hoping to get control and get me in all sorts of trouble."

IS IT POSSIBLE TO DO BETTER NEXT TIME?

Setting up preventive plans (for what you can do differently next time you are tempted to do something harmful or impulsive) takes us back to the incident in my office waiting room that I described at the beginning of this chapter. Is there some way that we could have prevented that incident from happening to my counseling client who allegedly got stared at and was made uncomfortable by one of my colleagues. Is there a process by which you can reduce the chances of painful moments like these before they occur?

So far in this chapter I've only described what happened in the waiting room from my counseling client's point of view. But near the end of that counseling session on the day she said she was stared at for far too long by one of my colleagues, I asked her how I might support what she wanted to do next about what had happened.

My client thought for a moment and replied, "I don't really want to file a complaint with the licensing board. I also don't want to have to talk with this invasive guy and educate him or rehabilitate him on what's a creepy stare versus what's an o.k. glance that doesn't make someone self-conscious or uncomfortable. I'm here to work on my own counseling issues and the grieving process about my kid sister--not to be this awkward guy's coach or mentor."

As we discussed various options for what to do next, we discovered that what she wanted most of all is for me to take some pro-active steps to make sure that what happened to her would not happen to anyone else in the future in that waiting room.

She explained, "I hope you can make an impact on this insensitive therapist and also for the rest of the people who work in this suite of offices. If you are willing, I'd be happy to sign some official-looking piece of paper and, as long as you keep my name and private information a secret, I would give you permission to talk with the creep and explain to him why it's not appropriate to stare at the chest of someone who is waiting for a counseling session. I'd also like you to talk with your other colleagues about how to make sure the waiting room is a safe place for women and also for men to know they aren't going to be hit on or glared at by any of the therapists."

The day after she signed a written release form to give me permission to discuss the incident without revealing her name or any identifying details, I set up a meeting with the red-haired therapist and some separate meetings with the therapists in the suite. The meetings with the other therapists were easy. They were each glad to be discussing the topic of how to make sure clients in the waiting room felt safe and how to make sure we alerted each therapist and staff member of the need to respect the privacy, integrity, and the sexual boundaries of each of the clients who came for counseling.

But the first conversation with the red-haired therapist wasn't so easy. He claimed at first he didn't recall the incident. When I refreshed his memory with some details, he changed his tune a little bit, but then he said defensively, "Why are you so sure she's the one who's telling the truth? I don't understand why my side of the story holds such little importance."

I told him I was very open to hearing if he had a different recollection of what happened or what it meant. But when I invited him again to tell his side of the story, he got silent. He said he was going to have to think about it and get back to me.

"Yikes," I thought to myself. "That was one defensive reaction. I do hope he can open up and be a little more honest the next time we meet."

A few days later we tried again. I started by saying, "I realize that the conversation we had the other day was very uncomfortable and possibly felt like a surprise attack. Is there anything I can do to help us get back on track toward coming up with ways to make sure our clients feel safe in the waiting room from now on."

My colleague was silent for almost ten seconds. It was a long ten seconds. Then he admitted, "I don't have a perfect memory. But I do know that if I'm going to be honest and real with myself and with you, then I have to admit that I do like to stare sometimes. My wife has pointed it out to me. My ex-wife commented on it several times. One of my male friends also said to me once, 'Hey, you ought to take a photograph…it'll last longer.' I guess I grew up at a time when you could get away with that stuff and no one called you out for it."

I thanked him for his honesty and asked him what he thought would make the waiting room a safe place for every type of client. He took a deep breath and I could see he was starting to get less defensive. He spoke softly as he admitted, "I didn't intend to hurt that young woman or make her uncomfortable. But it makes sense that being stared at for that many seconds is going to make someone feel rather weird and unsafe."

He then offered, "I'm willing to have you say we've talked and that you can tell her I am truly sorry for not being respectful and for making her uncomfortable at a place where she should be able to be unguarded and treated well. I'm also willing to catch myself the next time my eyes start to roam and to make sure I don't go farther than a quick glance so that I don't start acting like a perv."

Then he got a little bit fidgety in his chair as he said quickly with strong emotion, "I've trained for many years to be able to help people and I've worked for a long time to become successful with a full load of clients and to be able to support my family. I don't want to risk it all for the chance to stare at someone's body and make someone uncomfortable. That would be stupid and I'm not stupid. It wasn't easy growing up as the kind of brainy, short kid who was real awkward trying to find a relationship. I think I feel that when I stare at someone's body I'm somehow making up for all the times I was too shy or too nerdy to be able to get much attention from that kind of really attractive woman when I was in high school or college. But I don't want to hurt anyone and I certainly don't want to be the next guy written up in the newspaper getting busted by someone who catches him doing something inappropriate. That would be a huge mistake."

I saw in that moment that my colleague was both a highly-intelligent person with a desire to help and also an insecure and vulnerable person with a lingering problem that could still get him in a lot of trouble. I hope the conversation we had that day and a few other conversations we had over the next several months made a difference. But there's never a guarantee of whether an accuser will experience a complete healing or whether an accused person will experience a complete transformation of the barely-conscious motivation that caused him to act out inappropriately. There's so much more we all need to do to address the issues raised by the #MeToo movement and I hope we can address those issues together as compassionate allies rather than taking shots at each other as entrenched adversaries.

Chapter Three:

WHAT GETS ON YOUR NERVES WHEN PEOPLE TALK ABOUT ISRAEL

In the current decade, some specific topics are quite likely to provoke intense disagreements and passionate feelings. For example, a few years ago I heard about an interesting speaker regarding Israel who was going to talk at a local synagogue. I called a friend and we went to the talk, which had a packed audience of Jewish folks from all age groups and points of view.

It turned out to be a lot more than a speech. After just a few minutes, it started to resemble a Las Vegas mudwrestling brawl. Several people kept interrupting the speaker. Others were shouting obscenities at the interrupters.

Lots of insults and name-calling flew across the room like drone bombs. One of the shouters was denouncing "the idiots who endorse everything Israel does even when Israel is making mistakes." A different shouter was denouncing "the idiots who condemn Israel even when Israel is justified and using restraint." The person who had invited and introduced the speaker took the microphone and threatened to call the police.

I asked myself, "Is this where we've arrived in our ability to talk about the intricacies of Israel?"

Or as one of my relatives (who was in four concentration camps from the age of 16 to the age of 20) used to say sarcastically when he saw Jews yelling at each other, "For this I survived Auschwitz?"

During the next several pages, I will be exploring with you one of the most explosive, emotional, and divisive topics currently driving wedges between Jews. I won't be telling you what to think or which way to side on various controversies relating to Israeli government policies and Middle East peace possibilities. But I will be offering you several different ways to restore the mutual civility and compassion to the way we talk about Israel in our families, our places of worship, and other public forums and community events with Jews and non-Jews who agree or disagree with each other.

I've noticed especially in the past ten years that there's something toxic and dangerous happening. I first began to notice it when I would be invited to speak at various temples, synagogues, and book fairs across the United States and in each city there would be at least one rabbi, religious school teacher, non-profit board member, or congregational leader who would come up to me in a private moment and whisper to me, "We need help. In recent months, we can't seem to talk about Israel without a huge argument or a shouting match breaking out. It seems to be getting worse and the bitterness and resentments between people who disagree with each other about Israel are becoming more intense and irreconcilable."

I've also listened during dozens of counseling sessions in my office in the past few years where family members are at odds with each other because a dinner table discussion about Israel (often with a teen or young adult family member who has very different feelings about Israel than the parents or grandparents do) turned into a tense conversation or a screaming match. It saddens me each time I hear about siblings, business partners, close friends, or multi-generational families who love each other but are becoming estranged from one another because of how hard it is to talk about various controversies regarding Israel.

Is there someone in your own life right now who gets on your nerves because this person is so adamantly loyal to each recent Israeli prime minister, or so adamantly opposed to each recent Israeli prime minister? Is there someone you see at family gatherings, work events, or congregational events who makes your nerves catch fire when he or she starts talking about the situation in the Middle East?

THE TWO WOMEN WHO SHARED A SHABBAT PODIUM

If you are wondering, "Will these clashes about Israel ever get resolved successfully," I want to explore with you some new and creative ways to improve how we talk with each other and seek solutions together. Let's start with something highly successful that happened in the congregation where I've been attending services for the past 15 years. It might give you some good ideas for your own family gatherings, your own work setting, or your own congregation.

It started out as a regular Shabbat service. The usual prayers, the usual melodies, the familiar faces.

But something unforgettable and unique happened. During the reading of the weekly Torah portion, I found out that two women from the congregation had prepared and were going to give a creative teaching in which they would be inhabiting the roles of two powerful women in the biblical narrative.

The Torah portion that week was Va-yeira (which means "and He appeared") from Genesis Chapter 21 in which Sarah, the matriarch of the Jewish people, is clashing with Hagar, the matriarch of the Arab people. Here's the back story that will help you understand what happened:

In the previous week's Torah portion, Sarah and Hagar are quite close and trusting of one another. It says in Genesis 16:1 that Sarah was having trouble conceiving offspring and she urged her husband Abraham to conceive a child with Hagar, an Egyptian woman who works for them. Sarah's vulnerable words to Abraham in the Torah are: "Look, the Eternal One has kept me from bearing. Consort with my maid; perhaps I shall have a son through her." Sarah then "offers Hagar to her husband as a concubine and she (Hagar) conceived."

The two women from our congregation who were role-playing the words and feelings of Sarah and Hagar then began to dialogue with each other about how they had loved and relied on one another for many years. Both Sarah and Hagar felt they were "family" with each other. They were so close and trusting, they imagined it might be possible to remain as "family" forever.

But the plot begins to twist and get more complicated in the Torah portion after that. As soon as Hagar becomes pregnant with Abraham's child, there now is tension arising between Sarah and Hagar. According to the Torah narrative, Sarah fears that "Hagar seems to be feeling superior (or at an advantage) toward the childless Sarah" and Hagar fears that Sarah no longer appreciates or cares for Hagar.

Which brings us to what happens next in the current week's Torah portion Va-yeira. Sarah urges Abraham to send away Hagar and the child Ishmael (who is Abraham's first born son, conceived and raised with Hagar). The Torah description reveals that Abraham's second son (this time conceived with Sarah) is Isaac and it says in the Book of Genesis that the Israelite inheritance begins with Isaac and the descendants of Isaac (which includes all of the Jews living today).

The Torah in Genesis also teaches that there is a covenant between the Eternal One and Hagar and Abraham's son Ishmael that the Arab nations which emerge from that lineage will also be "a multitude of nations" (Genesis 17:4).

Now the two women playing the roles of Sarah and Hagar had shifted into a less trusting and more guarded way of discussing their differing feelings and experiences. The first woman from our congregation, the one portraying Sarah, talked about how anxious she felt that Hagar and Ishmael were mocking Sarah's son Isaac and that Hagar and Ishmael seemed unwilling to recognize the special relationship that Sarah, Abraham, Isaac, and Isaac's descendants had with the Eternal One. The woman from our congregation who was portraying Hagar also talked about how she felt equally anxious because she sensed that Sarah and Isaac and Isaac's descendants were not going to give respect or equal value to the covenant that Hagar and Ishmael have with the Eternal One.

According to the two women who were our Torah teachers that day, Hagar and Sarah both probably longed for the earlier, trusting relationship they had previously enjoyed and they both felt sad that it had turned into mistrust and anger. A mistrust and anger that lasted for thousands of years, even into the 21st century.

At this point in the Torah portion discussion on this particular Shabbat, the two women from our congregation began to describe their own differing life experiences and perspectives as modern-day Jews. The woman who was portraying Hagar spoke first and told us about her own lived experience growing up as a Jewish Israeli woman in Haifa with Arab neighbors, Arab school mates, Arab colleagues, and Arab dinner guests who helped her see the importance of understanding and appreciating the Arab point of view and the Palestinian point of view whenever there was a discussion or a policy decision to be made about Israel and the Palestinians. This well-educated and passionate Israeli-American woman who was portraying Hagar told us about her current life teaching at a rabbinic school near downtown Los Angeles. She feels her love for Israel is not diminished by her caring for the Arab and Palestinian points of view that she acquired as a child in Haifa and that she continues to develop as a human rights activist in Los Angeles.

The second woman from our congregation, the one who was portraying Sarah, then spoke about her own lived experience growing up in a small village near Jaffa and Tel Aviv. She described how she had shifted over the years to becoming more guarded and cautious about the possibility of peaceful co-existence with Arabs and Palestinians after she experienced several traumatic incidents in which friends and loved ones were attacked by terrorists in Israel. She told us she still had a small glimmer of hope that there might someday be a viable two-state solution, but mostly she feels the Palestinian and Arab leadership will probably fall short of recognizing and protecting the need for Israelis to have safety and security. This second woman from our congregation is also a well-educated and passionate Israeli-American who has taught at a different rabbinic school on the west side of Los Angeles. Her love for Israel and her efforts to protect Israel are two of the highest priorities in her life.

So here in front of us we were listening in real time and asking questions of two very well-informed and passionate Israeli-born women who had strongly different ideas on what to do about the dilemmas in Israel and the Middle East. Yet the substantial differences in their life experiences and political viewpoints did not result in any name-calling or in a disrespectful tone or attitude whatsoever.

What we discovered at this Torah teaching and discussion with two women portraying Sarah and Hagar is that there can be genuine emotional closeness and divergence of opinions at the same time. These highly-intelligent and caring women were willing and able to listen and honor the differing life experiences and beliefs of the other. It was not a fight or a competition we were witnessing at this Torah teaching, but rather a healthy forum for seeing two very different ways of addressing the same dilemma.

I felt so moved and impressed not just by the life stories and political ideas the two women were offering, but also by the caring tone and mutual support they had for each other. At the end of that unforgettable Torah discussion, both of the women agreed that seeking peace in the Middle East and a healthy democracy in Israel will need to include a deep understanding of both what Sarah and her descendants are feeling and what Hagar and her descendants are feeling. The jigsaw puzzle of what to do in Israel might require each diverse puzzle piece to be taken seriously and included in the decision-making process.

WHAT IS THE SECRET SAUCE FOR A CONVERSATION ABOUT ISRAEL THAT DOESN'T GO OFF THE RAILS

Please note that these kinds of civil and mutually-compassionate discussions don't happen by accident. There are specific things you and I need to do in order to increase the chances that a true sharing of ideas will occur and to reduce the chances that a mudwrestling disaster will disrupt your holiday meal, your Shabbat dinner table, your conversation with your kids or grandkids, or your discussions about Israel where you work or where you attend services.

What are these steps for pro-actively bringing out the best in people and helping them not go bonkers on each other?

In 2018 there was an extremely-successful 6-part series of lectures and discussions about Israeli and Palestinian history, culture, priorities, conflicts, and options for peace held at our congregation in West Los Angeles.

It had a large number of people attending—some from our medium-sized congregation and many from other parts of the city. All of us were nervous ahead of time that this 6-part series might get upended by the kinds of arguments and name-calling we had seen at other events.

But this time we discovered it's quite possible, even in these contentious and polarized times, to set up a healthy conversation and a creative sharing of innovative solutions. I asked my friend Jean Katz, the woman who had organized and was in charge of the logistics for this well-run 6-part series, "What exactly did you do that worked so effectively this time around? Is there a secret sauce, a pro-active way to avoid the kind of bitterness and tensions we have seen so often at prior events?"

Jean explained that based on her many years as a consultant and strategic planning facilitator for a large, contentious school district that often had divisive and explosive planning meetings, "I learned what to do ahead of time to increase the likelihood of a productive, problem-solving meeting rather than a disastrous shouting match where a few hot-heads are able to hijack the meeting and leave everyone frustrated. I discovered that three pro-active steps ahead of time can make a huge difference." Her three steps are:

Step One: Making sure there is a clear kavanah (or higher intention or mindfulness ground-rules) verbalized at the start of each session and repeated at the beginning of any question or feedback portion of the meeting.

Jean recalled, "I learned years ago that I can't expect anyone else to take care of this crucial step of setting the tone and the deeper purpose for what we are about to do in a large meeting where there are clashing points of view. I now make sure to say calmly and supportively that each of us is here at this meeting to learn something we don't already know, that each of us is here to listen to viewpoints we don't usually hear or agree with, and that each of us has a sacred responsibility to make this a welcoming, safe environment for genuine dialogue and mutual respect, even when we disagree with what someone is saying."

This kavanah or intention to have an open space for hearing lots of different points of view without interrupting or attacking anyone is not the same as a debate, a competition, or a rushed decision-making vote. Rather, it is a chance to listen with an open heart, to hear the feelings and experiences of the other, and to appreciate the diverse pieces of the puzzle we are trying to solve together.

As Jean and many other strategic planning consultants have found repeatedly over the years, "It's crucial to say out loud at least a few times during each session what the tone and ground-rules are, so that participants feel safe to offer their good ideas and no one gets trashed or shut down for having a view that differs from the majority."

Step Two: Making sure the speakers and the other facilitators demonstrate by their actions and their tone of voice that they, too, are willing to hear differing viewpoints and innovative hybrid solutions.

The organizer of the event or the person introducing the event can't do it alone. There needs to be an agreed-upon respectful tone (and an avoidance of provocative phrases or attitudes) modeled by each of the speakers and facilitators in order for genuine dialogue and brainstorming to occur.

This means you may need to talk ahead of time one-on-one with each of the individuals who will be attending your holiday meal, your upcoming Shabbat, or your congregation's discussion event. You may need to ask each person directly, "Out of respect for the hosts and the diverse people who will be attending, can I count on you to live up to the plan to treat each participant with respect and caring, even if you don't like what that person says or believes? Can I rely on you to set a tone of decency even when you start to feel a little heated inside your head?"

Quite often people need to know ahead of time that this is not a debate, a competition, or a winner-take-all fight for survival. Rather, this is a chance for people of differing views to come together to share a variety of ideas and perspectives, so that each participant will be more aware of the complexities and intricacies than they were previously.

Step Three: Give people the chance to speak and be heard in small well-facilitated break-out groups that report back to the larger group.

If there will be more than 10 people in the room, it's extremely helpful to break up into smaller sub-groups of 4 or 8 individuals for 10 or 20 minutes to allow each individual to have a chance to speak and then each sub-group can report back to the large group with ideas and challenges that came up in the sub-group break-out sessions. Each small break-out group should have a facilitator or two who is trained to be welcoming of diverse viewpoints and who can gently but firmly make sure no one gets interrupted or attacked when it's their turn to speak. It also helps to have one person take notes of what each person says and then either the note-taker or another individual can quickly review the notes and be the one who presents to the larger group what was said in this smaller group.

What you don't want is for people to feel like a pressure cooker about to explode because they fear they are not going to get a chance to speak. The break-out portion into smaller sub-groups can create a safe place where each individual will have two or three minutes of being heard and taken seriously.

There is still no 100% guarantee that a few hot-heads won't find a way to say something hurtful or dismissive toward someone else. But the chances are much higher of a healthy discussion and a productive brainstorming that includes multiple viewpoints if you include these three steps for helping people focus on "learning something new" rather than simply "clobbering people with what you already insist is the one and only solution."

As one participant at the recent 6-part lecture series and discussion told me, "I was worried ahead of time because I hate to see people yelling at each other and not listening to one another. But I was pleasantly surprised this time because there was a tone of genuine curiosity for each of the very different ideas offered by the diverse speakers and the wide variety of audience members. At each of the six sessions, I felt like I was in a room of passionate, committed people who have very different life experiences and unique insights into the possible solutions for Israel and the Middle East. It gave me hope that if we can listen to each other, then we can work together for what we all want: peace, prosperity, and mutual respect."

WHEN THE TENSIONS ABOUT ISRAEL THREATEN TO TEAR APART YOUR OWN FAMILY

For many American Jews, the clashes about Israel have become very personal and painful. One example is a highly-educated family I learned about because I was working with one of the family members, a sandwich-generation mom named Rhonda who came in for counseling to discuss her difficulties with her highly-opinionated aging parents and her highly-opinionated teenage daughter.

Rhonda is a trained speech therapist in her late 40's whose 18 year old daughter Ellie recently went on a supervised trip to Israel with a large number of college students from nearby schools and also from schools throughout North America and Europe. According to Rhonda, "I had thought this would be a good idea for Ellie to help her deepen her Jewish identity and her feelings for Israel. My parents (Ellie's grandparents) are very religious and devoted to Israel. My ex-husband and I are less religious but also supportive of Israel most of the time."

Rhonda's face became sad as she described, "What we didn't anticipate is that this trip to Israel has resulted in Ellie becoming somewhat alienated from her Jewishness. We aren't sure exactly what happened on the trip, but we think there were some incidents where Ellie and some of her friends got into a shouting match with the trip leader. Ellie came home with her mind made up, 'I don't want you ever to force me to do anything like this again.'"

Rhonda continued, "At a High Holiday dinner with Ellie's grandparents a few weeks after Ellie returned home, I was horrified when Ellie spoke out in favor of some of the ideas of the boycott/divest groups on her campus who are opposed to Israeli policies. The conversation got very heated and Ellie was quite vehement in telling her grandparents how angry she was about what she had experienced on her trip to Israel."

The next day, Ellie's grandparents were so upset, they told Rhonda that they were thinking about no longer paying for Ellie's expensive college tuition and housing costs. Rhonda's parents had always said they would help out and pay for Ellie's education, especially since Rhonda's ex is not helping very much. But with this family clash about Israel, Rhonda said, "I don't know what's gonna happen about this year's tuition. I also don't know how to repair the hurt feelings between Ellie and her grandparents."

As a therapist, I realized there were several challenging issues happening at once for Rhonda. One issue was how to deal with her 18 year old daughter Ellie. Another issue was how to deal with Rhonda's hurt and upset parents. A third issue was what to do about the current clash over whether Ellie's intense viewpoints since the Israel trip were going to result in continued clashes for Rhonda and her family.

Like many families where there are differing, passionate opinions about Israel, it was no longer just political. It had become a mine field threatening to explode each phone call, each Shabbat dinner, and each holiday get-together.

LISTENING WITHOUT LECTURING

Over the next several weeks, Rhonda worked hard in therapy to come up with effective ways to navigate the tensions in her family. She then spent some time listening compassionately to her parents describe how much they cared about Israel and how upset they were with the positions Ellie had taken at the holiday dinner. Rhonda also spent some time listening to her daughter Ellie and finding out exactly what had happened on the Israel trip that had caused Ellie to become so upset.

One of the things Rhonda discovered as a result of truly listening to her daughter's feelings is that Ellie's close friend from college, an outspoken activist named Julie, had tried several times to contradict the trip leader and had gotten into some fiery debates with the staff members and participants.

According to Ellie, "My friend Julie was treated badly by the people running the tour. They cut her off repeatedly. They refused to hear any opposing viewpoints. They said no whenever Julie tried to add some alternative sites to the tour so that we could see a different side of the story. The trip leaders seemed terrified of anything that would diverge from the rigid narrative they were presenting."

What Rhonda also discovered during an additional late-night conversation with her daughter Ellie is that Ellie's friend Julie had shown up on the trip with the secret agenda to agitate and disrupt the trip leader and the particular viewpoint that the trip leader was favoring. Ellie admitted, "My friend Julie had signed up for the trip with the single purpose of shaking things up and had been coached ahead of time by an organization that is known on campus to be strongly opposed to Israeli policies. I think Julie spent several months getting trained on how to provoke and upset the people who organized the trip."

During her next counseling session, Rhonda thought about how to respond to Ellie's openness and willingness to admit to Rhonda that Ellie's friend Julie had been secretly trained to disrupt the trip. As Rhonda explained to me, "Usually an 18 year old is going to side with her friend and keep things from a nosy parent. I appreciate that Ellie could have kept this from me and I don't want to lose her trust. I wish there were some way to help Ellie make up her own mind and not be so swayed by her friend Julie."

Near the end of that counseling session, Rhonda came up with a sensible idea on what to do next to keep the lines of communication open with her daughter. Rhonda decided to sit down with Ellie and brainstorm together about how to do a better job than Julie had done for making changes in the policies and narratives of the trip leader and his staff.

During a relaxed and gentle two-way conversation, Rhonda asked Ellie, "Instead of just provoking the trip leader and making a scene that caused him to become defensive and angry, what are some better options for being a positive change agent? If we think about it, what might be a possible way to influence and encourage the tour leaders and staff for opening up the conversation and being more inclusive of alternative viewpoints and sites?"

This open-hearted, non-pressuring question from Rhonda to her daughter Ellie seemed to get Ellie interested in exploring various options. Ellie thought for a few moments and then replied, "I'm not sure about the trip leader, who was somewhat of a jerk, but I do have some hope for three of his staff members who confided to me in private that they also would prefer a more balanced and diverse way of discussing the issues and honoring the many Israeli points of view and the many Palestinian and Arab Israeli points of view."

For the next several days, Ellie and Rhonda began to work together to write a few letters and make a few calls to some of the program staff, the fundraising directors, and board members of the organization that had sponsored the Israel trip. They didn't know if they were going to get a reply or make an impact, but they decided to give it a try and see what happened.

While working together on these letters and phone calls, Rhonda explained to Ellie, "This feels very Jewish to me that instead of running away from a complicated situation, we're attempting to do something to repair it. One of the things I love most about being Jewish is that we are repeatedly encouraged to ask questions and seek to improve what's broken or unfair. I wasn't on the trip with you, but I can hear from your stories that something was not quite balanced or fair about the way they dealt with questions and differing viewpoints. I truly believe that there will be at least a few individuals in the organization that sponsored the trip who want to hear your questions and your suggestions if you talk to them from a place of respect and decency."

Ellie was a bit skeptical, saying, "I don't know if these letters and phone calls are going to do much. Especially if the donors and board members only want one side of the story to be presented."

Over the next few weeks, Ellie began to change her mind somewhat when she heard from several of the program staff and two of the board members that they were taking her suggestions seriously and that Ellie was not the only trip alum who had spoken out in a caring and respectful way, which they deeply appreciated.

One of the board members spent over an hour on the phone with Ellie listening to what happened on the Israel trip and brainstorming with Ellie on what could be done to make sure that on future trips there would be a stronger sense of mutual respect and good listening to the various points of view. This board member commented, "There is so much diversity of opinion in Israel and so many differing ideas on how to improve things. Please don't ever feel that your ideas and your insights are to be suppressed or kept from us. I want you to promise to call me whenever you have additional suggestions that we need to hear."

From her friend Julie before and during the trip, Ellie had assumed there were only two possible options: "Are you for Israel or are you for the Palestinians and Israeli Arabs?" But from her conversations with several people after the trip and from reading a variety of writers on the complex history and personal lives of numerous Israelis, Palestinians, and Israeli Arabs, Ellie slowly began to realize that there were many individuals and groups currently speaking up who had fascinating ideas on how to secure human rights, personal safety, and improved living conditions for all those who are attempting to live together or side-by-side in peace.

As Ellie admitted to her mom one afternoon when they were taking a walk together at a nearby park, "I was told by Julie that the Israel trip leaders were never going to budge, but I've found that the majority of people we've contacted are quite willing to explore the complex issues and be open to intense discussions and alternative points of view. It makes me want to keep learning more and not shutting my eyes to any of the realities. There's so much more I need to understand."

A few days later, Rhonda visited with her parents and she recalls, "It took a while for my mom and dad to realize that Ellie's inquisitive mind is not something to be afraid of, but rather something to invest in and nurture. That was what my own parents taught us each year at the Passover Seders they led, which said repeatedly that asking questions and seeking freedom and dignity for all people are very essential Jewish values. I realized that Ellie is not leaving her Jewishness, but living her Jewishness because she's willing to dig deep and ask the questions that need to be asked."

Chapter Four:

ARE THERE RED VS. BLUE TENSIONS IN YOUR LIFE LATELY?

Can we talk about politics without angering each other?

I'll be honest: When I was a kid growing up in Detroit, everyone I knew was a Democrat. The first time I saw a Republican up close happened at a United Way volunteers' dinner downtown. The clothing store where my father worked had sent my dad to the volunteers' dinner and he took me along because my mom was in the hospital.

I saw a well-dressed and articulate man named Max Fisher give a speech about why he cared so much about charities that empowered people to lift themselves out of poverty. I found out that night from my father that every time there has been a Republican president (Eisenhower, Nixon, Ford, Reagan, Bush, etc), this wealthy entrepreneur from Detroit, Max Fisher, would be called in as a trusted advisor.

My father said softly to me so no one else could hear, "When I was growing up in Germany, no one on the inside could speak up for Jewish or humanitarian causes. But in America, Max Fisher stands up for us when there's a Republican in the White House. We need someone they'll listen to." My father would never vote for a Republican, but he was glad there was a Max Fisher who could call the President, the Governor, or the Mayor and say, "Here's something important you need to consider."

Ironically, it was Max Fisher's daughter Mary Fisher who opened my eyes to another example of why Republican Jews, Democratic Jews, and Independent Jews need one another. In 1992, the Republican party was under a lot of pressure and criticism because of how harsh and unsupportive they had been toward people with AIDS. At the Republican National Convention in Houston, Texas in 1992, Max Fisher's daughter Mary Fisher got up on the podium on national television and gave a memorable speech about how she contracted AIDS from her ex-husband and how she was coping with the uncertainty of whether AIDS research would ever find the right medicines to prolong life or obtain a cure.

She also spoke in detail on how Republicans nationwide needed to support certain policies that could save tens of thousands of lives that were at risk. The convention burst into applause and several legislators shifted their positions to support more funding for AIDS research and treatment. Mary Fisher's speech to her fellow Republicans was later ranked as one of the 50 most important American speeches of the 20th century. Looking back, I tend to think "Maybe my immigrant dad was correct. Maybe there needs to be compassionate Jews on several sides of each complicated American issue so that people will be listened to during a time of clashing viewpoints and angry divisiveness."

It's been 28 years since Mary Fisher spoke up about AIDS funding. She's still alive today, but the intense polarization and distrust between Republicans, Democrats and Independents has gotten much worse during these 28 years. It's become extremely difficult to find common ground on issues when each side is so locked into rigid positions and bad feelings about anyone who holds a different viewpoint.

In your own life and holiday dinners, what's it like lately? Are there clashes between Democrats, Republicans, and Independents that cause heated arguments or cold stares between people at work, at family dinners, in your congregation, or even in a parking lot when someone in a red "Make America Great Again" hat is vying for a parking spot with someone who is wearing a "Feel the Bern" or a "Black Lives Matter" t-shirt.

Right now in the not-so-united states of America, we've got a deluge of Russian bots on our cell phones and laptops that are provoking us to fight with one another and we've got adrenalin rushing through our nervous system that causes us to heat up quickly whenever we think the other side of the U.S. political divide is about to pull something on us. The tension has risen to a much higher level than at any time since the Civil War. Can we hold it together if the divisiveness continues to worsen?

WHY WE HAVE SO MUCH TROUBLE EXCHANGING IDEAS WITH EACH OTHER

I've heard and read dozens of theories as to why we are so short-fused and easily-agitated on numerous political issues. But my favorite and least complicated theory was explained to me several years ago when I sat next to a woman from Belgium in her mid-20's on an airplane ride from Chicago to New York. This woman, who was studying for an advanced degree in Media Communications Management, had been living in the United States for almost two years and she said to me calmly, "You Americans are really strange."

I said, "What do you mean?"

She replied, "In Europe we have actual journalists and actual news programs that do a lot of legwork to find out several sides of a complicated issue. In the United States, you've got a small number of big corporations making a lot of money by having what looks like news programs but they are actually partisan preaching platforms where every day they get people all worked up and angry about a few particular issues. They make their money by getting people terrified and angry of the opposing point of view. They make it very hard for people to have a reasonable conversation about the complexities and various ways of solving an important situation. I feel sad that you folks are at each other's throats. You are a great country and free speech is a wonderful thing. But both your left wing media and your right wing media have gotten into a rut of demonizing the other side and having no patience to hear the various sides of an issue. It's very sad."

I thought of that Belgian woman recently when I was having lunch with a consultant friend my wife and I have known for over 20 years. This woman who is a brilliant consultant has been kind and open-minded to us and to our child who has special needs. She is like "family" and we have cared about each other's families through all sorts of changes and crises during these 23 years.

But it's always a little delicate and uncomfortable to talk about politics with this woman because she lives in Orange County and watches Fox News, while we live near what many refer to humorously as the Peoples Republic of Santa Monica and we are addicted to watching Rachel Maddow almost every night.

In the middle of a pleasant lunch, if this woman brings up the issue of immigration policy, I discover almost immediately in the conversation that her mind has been filled recently with terrifying stories on Fox News about gangs from Central America who allegedly are raping and murdering people after they enter the United States, while my mind has been filled recently with terrifying stories on CNN and MSNBC about seemingly innocent asylum seekers being separated at the U.S. border from their infant and toddler children. We are being fed two completely different stories and both of these divergent narratives cause us to feel horrified that "the other side is clueless about the truth of what's going on."

Both this woman and I are compassionate people, yet it's difficult to explore the accuracy of each other's viewpoints because we are so filled with horrific stories about how insensitive and misinformed the "other side" tends to be. Is it possible for the two of us to talk with one another without one or both of us thinking silently, "How could someone so intelligent be so mistaken about something that is so obvious?" Are we even talking about the same thing when one of us is being told the issue is completely about murderers entering our country and the other one of us is being told the issue is completely about moms and kids being split apart from each other instead of being guided on a legal path to full citizenship.

APPRECIATING THAT BOTH SIDES FEEL UNHEARD AND FRUSTRATED

If you step back for a moment and listen to what each of the sides of the political divides are saying, you can begin to hear the pain that so many people are feeling today. Here are just a few examples of what I have heard recently from friends, relatives, and therapy clients. See if these sound like what you've experienced in your own life these past few years:

- At Thanksgiving dinner in November 2016, one of my counseling clients watched in horror when one of her Trump-supporting relatives and one of her Trump-hating relatives got into an ugly shouting match. Everyone in the room felt extremely uncomfortable as the name-calling and the angry accusations kept escalating. It has caused most of the family members to take sides and be at odds with each other ever since. Both sides seem to be saying, "Why don't you stop calling me names and start listening to my legitimate reasons why I feel the way I do about the current situation." Yet neither side is willing to budge.

- Two of my work colleagues (one is a long-time progressive and the other is a long-time moderate) are embroiled in a continuing bitter feud. They were upset with each other in 2000 when one of them supported Nader and the other wanted Gore. Their bitterness flared up again in 2015 and 2016 (when these two individuals were arguing constantly in the hallway and on social media about Bernie versus Hillary). This clash between these two passionate and well-educated individuals not only has been causing all sorts of tensions and gossip at work and on social media, but it also has a lot of people worrying about the 2020 elections and whether there will be sufficient unity or unhealed gripes once someone is nominated.

- One of my cousins is a conservative Republican/Libertarian who hates what he calls "government intrusiveness" and is passionately opposed to any health care law that includes giving financial breaks or free health care to lower-income citizens. This cousin has said to me and other family members several times with great emotion, "Why should I have to pay for someone else's medical care. That's not my responsibility and I resent your tone of voice when you accuse me of being heartless. I give to charities freely, but I will not be told by the Nanny State what to do."

- One of my other cousins is a strong advocate for subsidized health care for all. He feels, "Health care is a right, not a privilege. There is no good reason why the richest nation in history can't set up a system to make sure that middle class and lower income folks don't die or go bankrupt as a result of an unexpected illness."

- Several people in my extended family are convinced that the Republican Party is better at standing up against anti-Semitism.

- Several other people in my extended family are convinced that the Democratic Party is better at standing up against white nationalists and other anti-Semites.

- One of my friends from college likes to say, "You can't have a conversation with a Republican because they are unwilling to stand up to a dishonest and corrupt leader."

- One of my other friends from college likes to say, "You can't have a conversation with a Democrat because they are so self-righteous and emotional about even the smallest things like whether to sip from a plastic straw or whether to let anyone say anything that isn't politically correct."

A DIFFERENT WAY OF SEEING THE ISSUE

In order to make some progress at restoring some civility and teamwork between those who are Republicans, Democrats, and Independents, I want to offer you a Jewish perspective that might be helpful. It's not very complicated. But it will require you to be honest with yourself about the cocoons we live in and whether we are going to venture out to truly get to know those who see things differently.

Here's what I mean by a Jewish approach to the dilemma of clashing political viewpoints:

In Judaism, there is a daily, weekly, and yearly opportunity to "take an accounting of your soul, a Heshbon Ha-Nefesh." It just takes a few seconds or a few minutes to look closely to find your own blind spots and the places in your psyche where you tend to be out of balance between two seemingly opposite qualities. For example, each person can take an accounting about whether that day we have been a little out of balance leaning too much toward Hesed (responding to everything with unlimited kindness and caring) or whether we have been a little bit out of balance leaning too much toward Gevurah (responding to everything with rules, firmness, order, structures, limits).

To give you an idea of how Hesed (lovingkindness) and Gevurah (limit-setting, firmness) occurs in your own daily life, imagine a situation where your romantic partner, your child, or a friend calls you on the phone and asks for something. If you are 100% Hesed (lovingkindness) you probably will rush in and do whatever this person asks of you. You care, you want to help, and you have a huge desire to be of service to this person.

Or if you are 100% Gevurah (limit-setting, firm, orderly), you probably will look at your packed schedule and say, "Nope, not today. Not me." It's not that you don't care, but your priority as a Gevurah person tends to be sticking to the rules, sticking to the plan, sticking to the routines.

From a Jewish spiritual perspective, being 100% Hesed or 100% Gevurah is probably going to be a problem for you and the people in your life. If you are a Hesed person who is so generous and limitless in giving, giving, giving of your time, your attention, your caring, and your funds to each and every situation that tugs at your heart, you might find yourself running low on funds or running low on energy. You might hear yourself saying, "I feel as if I give so much to so many, and as a result I don't have much time or energy left for myself or some of my most important priorities and goals."

Or if you a Gevurah person who sticks to your routines and schedules at the expense of your loved ones who need your attention sometimes or your patient listening, you may find them pulling away from you or saying, "Why are you so rigid and unsupportive? Why can't you make room once in a while for some spontaneity, some quiet moments, some chances to connect without being on a tight schedule all the time?"

In the Jewish tradition of Musar (which means to use Jewish teachings to work on your character traits to find more balance in the areas where you are leaning heavily in one direction or another and it's costing you in your health or your relationships), you might want to consider moving a little toward the healthy balance between the extremes of 100% Hesed and 100% Gevurah. For instance, what if you spoke with or imagined some- one as your once-a-month or once-a-year guide who can give you ideas on how to shift slightly toward a successful blending of the best qualities of being Hesed (generous and kind) and the best qualities of being Gevurah (focused and structured)?

If you were to have a lunch or a walk once a month or once a year with someone who has the opposite style from yourself, you will probably find lots of ideas and methods for how to shift from 100% Hesed to 80% Hesed and soon be able to set limits lovingly (rather than coldly or rigidly). Or you might find lots of ideas and methods for how to shift from 100% Gevurah to 80% Gevurah and soon be able to open up and be more generous and kind (while still being able to set limits and stay focused). Wouldn't that be a great thing to be able to shift slightly and be the kind of person who can say yes to some spontaneity and generosity when it's appropriate and who can say no compassionately when someone or something is going to push you past your limits?

Now here comes the political part. If you are leaning in one direction or another on the political spectrum, you might need to talk with or imag- ine someone from the other side of the spectrum to be your once-a-month or once-a-year source of ideas on how to explore a healthy balance.

For instance, if you are a liberal Democrat who feels an urge to be 100% Hesed (generous and kind) to every cause and every bold progressive proposal, then imagine for a moment having a conversation with a conser- vative Republican or Libertarian who can give you some ideas of how to say no once in a while to something that costs too much or that is too pie- in-the-sky and probably won't have the intended results. I'm generalizing here, but if you sense that Democrats like to say yes to any and all ways to achieve progress and new solutions, while Republicans tend to say no to most attempts to spend money on new solutions, then a Democrat can still be generous and kind but also learn some of the skill sets Republicans have for saying "no" or "not yet" to things that might need a slower or less costly solution.

Or if you are a conservative Republican or Libertarian who doesn't think that government programs solve problems and you want to cut rather than spend, what if you have a conversation with a Democrat to hear if there are some programs and solutions that are well-designed and cost-efficient enough to merit your support. Even if you hate the idea of government regulations, are there some food safety concerns or clean water concerns that you would like to brainstorm about with a Democrat or an Independent to come up with a hybrid solution that has the best qualities of what a Democrat, an Independent, and a Republican can come up with if they put their heads together as teammates instead of adversaries.

Just like the Jewish Musar practice of learning from the other extreme so that you can find a healthy balance somewhere in between, so can people with political differences work together to balance out their different strengths and build on each other's ideas. Imagine for a moment how much progress and personal improvement could occur if we had respectful conversations between people who are politically diverse but were willing to share their skill sets with each other. For example:

- If you are a highly spontaneous independent person who doesn't like following rules or traditions, what if you went to lunch once a month or once a year with a very traditional and "by-the-book" person from work or from your extended family to simply get a feel for how this person creates some order, dependability, routines, and traditions. Rather than judging or resenting this person who is different from you, what if you explored whether there are any possible benefits you might bring to your own life from learning the nuts and bolts of how this person sets up structures, routines, and dependability in his or her life. You don't have to lose your independent spirit by having lunch and seeking to understand this person's skill set, but rather you will be giving yourself the possibility of learning how to shift 10% or 20% from the painful extreme of "my life is so spontaneous and chaotic, I miss out on all sorts of stability and dependability that I wish I could have some of the time." It's about moving toward balance while still thriving as a basically spontaneous and independent spirit.

• Or if you are a highly structured, "don't rock the boat," or "don't touch my routines" type of person, what if you took to lunch or had a conversation once a month or once a year with someone who lives with a lot more flexibility, creativity, joy and playfulness. You won't have to give up your structured ways entirely, but only to explore if there are a few spontaneous possibilities that might shift your style from being an extremely inflexible person to becoming the kind of "sometimes flexible and playful" individual your loved ones have hoped you might be some of the time.

• Or if you are someone who has never been given (or who has tossed aside) any system of belief, morality, or sense of connection to something beyond the human realm, what if you decided to have lunch or a no arm-twisting conversation every month or every year with someone from work or your extended family who lives with a tight and highly-structured system of belief, morality, or sense of connection to something beyond the human realm. You don't have to agree 100% or be pressured to shift to this person's way of believing and practicing their beliefs, but only to have a chance to ask yourself every so often, "If I were going to add just 10% or 20% more structure and sense of community to my personal search for meaning and purpose, what would it be?"

• Or if you are someone who has a lot of guilt, shoulds, obligations, and rigid beliefs, what if you went to lunch or a walk once a month or once a year with someone who has integrity and morals but doesn't have your same organized system of belief or religious practice? If you were to keep the best of your beliefs but to lighten up on the guilt, shoulds, obligations, and rigidities you've been experiencing, what would that look like in your own life and your own style?

Learning from "the other" and opening up to the possibility of finding a healthy balance in your own life is a powerful way to refine and enhance your own character traits. For many centuries, Jews have met in two-person hevruta (friendship) study partnerships or in Musar (character development) groups to look at what are the extremes we have fallen into and how do we achieve a healthier balance without losing the good parts of who we are.

SIGNS OF HOPE

This wild idea of having lunch or taking a walk once a month or once a year with someone from a different part of the political spectrum in order to expand your own skill set (without giving up your core beliefs or your essential way of being) is something that few people do these days, but I've found repeatedly that when someone does take the bold risk to listen to the other with an open heart some amazing things can happen. Here are a few examples to stir up your own ideas of who you might want to have lunch with once a month or once a year and who you might want to brainstorm with every so often about how to achieve more balance in life:

Example #1: WHAT TO DO ABOUT A LONGTIME FRIEND WHO IS YOUR OPPOSITE IN MANY WAYS

Lisa is a Jewish Democrat and Paula is a Jewish Republican who met years ago at a company where they both worked. They were there at each other's weddings. They were on the phone exchanging ideas when each of them was pregnant and when their kids were little. They also have been there for each other in dealing with the challenges of having aging parents who needed a lot from them.

But their friendship became somewhat strained during the Obama years when Lisa adored Obama and Paula hated him. The tension got worse when Trump was elected after Paula told Lisa how strongly Paula feels that, "My husband and I believe Trump is better for Israel and the economy."

Lisa told me in 2018 during one of her counseling sessions that, "I feel kinda horrified that someone as moral and intelligent as Paula can vote for someone like Trump. It's so depressing to see how he gets away with things and yet people are willing to put up with him because their 401k's have gone up in value." Whereas Lisa and Paula used to talk on the phone at least once a week and go to museums and art shows several times a year, the political differences were now causing them to drift apart to the extent that Lisa and Paula hadn't spoken or seen one another for almost ten months.

In Lisa's therapy, one of the central issues she wanted to explore was how to deal with the fact that Lisa had gone through a lot of losses in the past few years with her mom dying from Parkinson's and Lisa's daughter moving away to live with a new boyfriend who is very controlling and sometimes verbally abusive. Lisa told me during a counseling session, "I worry that I'm also losing my longtime friendship with Paula. I just can't see how the two of us can feel close and trusting again when we view the current political situation so completely opposite from each other."

Like many women and men I have counseled in the past few years, the political tensions between Lisa and Paula were threatening to take away an irreplaceable bond they had built with each other over many years and decades. According to Lisa, "I've always known that Paula and I are some-what different, but there was a lot of caring and shared history between us. I realize she likes traditional values and I like to explore new ways of being. She likes routines and stability. I tend to go for spontaneity and wonderful detours from the rigid plans. Paula expects her kids to toe the line and she tells them often what they need to do to keep her happy. I tend to let my kids follow their own inner guidance and sometimes that works great and sometimes, like with my daughter and her controlling boyfriend, I worry that it's not turning out the way I hoped."

We explored in counseling several ways to deal with the loss of Lisa's mom and the uncertainty about her daughter. We made a lot of progress in both of these areas in just a few months. But Lisa continued to feel a deep sadness about possibly cutting off from Paula entirely. She commented, "I have known Paula for many years and we share an important history with each other. We knew each other when we were both single. We knew each other when we were both pregnant. We knew each other when we were figuring out how to raise kids and juggle our careers as well. I don't have anyone else in my life, even my husband, who knows my story and my struggles the way Paula knows them. But I get this horrible feeling inside when I think of her politics. It's so hard to reconcile the friend I need and the awful things that come out of her mouth about her political beliefs."

I asked Lisa if she would be willing to have lunch with Paula once a month or once a year to try out an experiment. The experiment would be, "Is there some gift or talent that Paula has and this gift or talent might be useful for this next chapter of your own life? Is there something you would like to learn from Paula that is worth spending time with her even if her political views are not what you wish she would have?"

Lisa thought for a moment and then her eyes opened wide as she admitted, "I think the gift or talent I would want to learn from Paula is how she manages to get people together for dinners, holiday gatherings, and big events with so much regularity and success. I've always been the kind of person who stresses about having people over to my house and I usually don't have a plan or anything dependable lined up ahead of time for major holidays or group events on my days off. I guess I would want to learn how Paula creates so much structure, dependability, and sense of community in her life, even though I would still like to be much more spontaneous, flexible and creative than she is."

Now that Lisa had some ideas of what else besides politics might be discussed at their next lunch, Lisa took the next step. She called Paula to have lunch the following week and to ask Paula for the nuts and bolts details of how Paula plans, organizes, and avoids burnout, even when she has ten people over for a Shabbat dinner or thirty people over for a holiday, or a hundred people for a congregational event that Paula puts together at least once a year. At that lunch, Lisa directly asked Paula, "I would love for you to teach me how you arrange these dinners and gatherings so successfully and smoothly," which caused Paula to talk in detail about several tips and short-cuts that could help Lisa become much more adept at having people over to her home (and it steered the conversation away from the political topics that had caused so much friction in the past).

What Lisa discovered is that the same personality trait that helps Paula to be so organized and dependable as an event planner is also what makes Paula crave traditional values, rules, and routines. Lisa told me, "Paula loves structure and order. I've always run away from structure and order. But I realize now that I can learn a few tips about structure and order from Paula while still remaining my spontaneous, flexible, and adventurous self."

As Lisa found out from this and other lunches she had with Paula in which Paula was mentoring Lisa on how to throw dinner parties and large gatherings, "Learning a few of the skill sets from someone who is your opposite doesn't mean I'm going to lose my own style. It just means I can do my own spontaneous, playful style with some of the planning, structure, and logistical skills that someone like Paula uses with her more traditional crowd."

Example #2: THE DAD WHO LIGHTENED UP A LITTLE TOWARD HIS ANXIOUS KIDS.

Another example of how two people from opposite sides of the political spectrum can learn from one another is the story of a college friend of mine named Jonathan who has a sister named Carol. Jonathan is a very focused, disciplined and conservative finance expert who is extremely cautious about taking risks, while his younger sister Carol is an artist and school teacher who loves trying new foods, new fashion ideas, alternative spiritual paths, and creative ways of designing her home. For years, Jonathan and Carol didn't like each other and avoided one another, especially since Jonathan is a passionate Libertarian politically and Carol is a left-of-center Progressive.

Then a few months ago, Jonathan got called into his troubled 22 year old daughter's therapy session (with a therapist I have known for many years that I recommended to Jonathan and his wife when they called to ask for a referral).

As Jonathan told me on the phone the day after the therapy session, "I was on the hot seat most of the fifty minutes. My daughter and my wife described me to the therapist as this overly cautious, overly protective dad who is terrified of taking risks and always afraid of letting either one of them try new things or have fun. Can you believe I had to pay a hundred fifty dollars to the shrink so I could sit there and let my wife and daughter talk trash about me?"

We've known each other a long time and are very honest with one another, so I asked Jonathan, "And was that an accurate description of Jonathan the anxious dad?"

Jonathan laughed, "Yes, it was accurate. But what they didn't mention is that my cautious, conservative approach to money management and life in general is the reason our family is financially secure."

As we talked for several minutes on the phone, I realized that even though Jonathan was upset that he had been put on the hot seat by his daughter and his wife, he was also sensible enough to know that he might continue to be unable to reach his troubled daughter and drift farther apart from his wife if he didn't lighten up a little bit on how much cautiousness and overprotectiveness he'd been putting on his highly-creative kids. Like many hard-working, highly-disciplined individuals, Jonathan had been told repeatedly by his loved ones, "You need to loosen up a little." But he had refused to listen until he was put on the hot seat in the therapist's office for an uncomfortable fifty minutes.

Jonathan asked me, "I don't want to fail at this. Do you know where I could get some coaching on how to be more effective with my kids without becoming too permissive or letting them waste money on silly things."

I replied, "I'm going to say something that you are probably going to hate at first glance. But I want you to think about this."

He said, "Go for it, Mr. Shrink."

I offered, "I think you could learn a lot if you took your sister Carol out to lunch and asked her to teach you how to connect better with your creative kids and how to bring out the best in them. Carol's amazing at working with teens and young adults. She's won lots of awards for the creative ways she deals with diverse young people who need special attention and alternative ways of getting their life on track."

Jonathan responded, "You were right. I do hate that idea."

"That's okay. You can hate the idea and I know you can tell me that Carol is a bleeding heart do-gooder and all that. But she's definitely a gifted teacher and she knows the way to develop the strengths and the talents of so many different kinds of kids. You don't have to become Carol or agree with her views of the world. You just need to let her give you some of her hard-earned wisdom about how to engage and inspire a troubled young person and to help bring out the best in your daughter."

A few weeks later, Jonathan called me and admitted, "I was really pissed at you for suggesting I should go have some absurd kumbaya moment with my spacey younger sister. I still think Carol is a flake and is way out there politically. But she did teach me a few ways to get my kids and especially my 22 year old to talk to me and trust me to listen and care for them. More importantly, she told me some excellent things she has seen in my teenage daughter and how to bring out those talents rather than trying to force my daughter to be someone else who is more like me, her dad."

Jonathan concluded, "I'm not promising to have lunch with Carol too often because we are just so very different. But I did thank her for being willing to help me out of a jam this time. I don't want my daughter to fall apart more than she already has and even if it means calling Carol once in a while to get some suggestions, I'm willing to do that. I do not want to fail at this messy thing called being a dad."

Example #3: CAN PEOPLE GET BEYOND THEIR DIFFERENCES IN ORDER TO SAVE SOME LIVES?
I need to ask you a question that will possibly reveal your age. Do you remember the "Smoking Section" and the "Non-Smoking Section" on domestic airlines?

For any readers who are too young to recall the "Smoking Section" and the "Non-Smoking Section" during the 1970's and 1980's, picture this:

The smokers are puffing away in one section of the cramped narrow airplane cabin. The non-smokers are nonetheless breathing in dense smoke and chemicals through much of the flight.

A Jewish Senator from New Jersey named Frank Lautenberg (who was formerly a two-pack a day smoker) pointed to a series of scientific findings in 1986 from the National Academy of Sciences on the dangers of second-hand smoke and he asked the Senate Transportation Committee to ban smoking on domestic flights. People on both sides of the issue started screaming at each other. The smokers said, "You're taking away my rights." The non-smokers said, "Really???? On every flight I'm choking on your smoke. How about my rights?"

The airlines industry said, "If you regulate smoking on flights, you are compromising the safety on all flights because you will be forcing smokers to hide in the bathroom and sneak a smoke." The chairman of the Civil Aeronautics Board sided with the airlines executives as he declared, "I think non-smokers have rights, but it comes into market conflict with practicalities and the realities of life." Senator Jesse Helms, a Republican from the tobacco state of North Carolina, tried to stop the bill by filibustering (talking for hours on the Senate floor to force an end to the debate on the bill). President Reagan's Secretary of Transportation, Elizabeth Dole, insisted that we needed more research and that no bills should pass until there was a lot more proven beyond a doubt.

Watching this back-and-forth shouting match on television, I decided to go to lunch with a member of my extended family who is a Republican, a smoker, and someone who has worked as a legislative assistant to some top Republicans. Even though he and I disagree on all sorts of things, we've still been able to talk and work together taking care of our elderly relatives that we have in common. He also has a great sense of humor and we've always been able to joke with each other about political issues.

So I asked my devoutly conservative relative, "Would you be willing to explain to me why Transportation Secretary Elizabeth Dole, who seems like a nice, caring person, is trying to stop the effort to ban smoking on airplanes?"

My relative took a few puffs on his cigarette and then replied, "This is hard for most Democrats to understand, but the purpose of governing is not to jump ahead of the consensus and tell all the people that you are going to save them from themselves with unnecessary regulations or to keep them healthy by outlawing the things that people freely choose to do in a free country."

I said, "Okay, that part of the conservative belief system I do understand. You don't like regulations and you want companies to be free to do what they want if the market will say yes to it. But what about the research that says smoking kills people and that second-hand smoke is going to cause damage for kids, moms, and innocent bystanders."

My relative took a few more puffs on his cigarette and answered, "Do you have to be so emotional and self-righteous about everything? The way things happen in America are like this: If the companies find that the vast majority of people won't fly on a plane that has smoke-filled aisles, then the companies will decide to ban smoking. But government should only be the last resort and we don't need government to get involved with all sorts of excessive, permanent rules and interference, unless there is chaos or a drop in business profitability in that industry. Let the consumers in the marketplace rather than the government in their lofty offices tell the airlines when it's time to ban smoking. I assume you are going to think I'm being heartless and uncaring here since you Democrats are all worked up about some research that claims lives are at risk. But scientific studies are theories and government can't jump in with all sorts of excessive regulations and emotional craziness because of some theories or some trendy ideas."

I came away from that lunch thinking about the fact that my Republican relative did have an interest in avoiding "market chaos" and "drops in the companies' profitability."

Then a few weeks later, I found out that Senator Lautenberg from New Jersey and a young House member named Dick Durbin from Illinois were two Democrats who were having one-on-one discussions with Republican legislators to discuss the chaos and drops in profitability that were hitting the airlines industry as a result of the public debate about whether to ban smoking on flights and the confusion over which airlines were starting to ban smoking and which airlines were not.

As the chaos and drops in profitability got worse, additional Republican Senators and House members started to become involved in crafting with Lautenberg and Durbin a bill that successfully banned smoking on domestic flights and made it illegal to smoke in the bathrooms as well. It had been almost 25 years since people had begun to cite scientific research on the health dangers, but now there was a quick vote and the bill passed. Order and predictability had returned to the friendly skies. Numerous Republicans and most Democrats were comfortable with the new smoking ban.

A similar process played out 30 years later. Senator Frank Lautenberg in early 2013 tried to pass a bill that would outlaw a specific group of industrial chemicals and chemical products on store shelves that had been shown in scientific studies to cause severe health risks and fatalities. The Republicans and the chemical industry tried to block the legislation. Then after Lautenberg died in June of 2013, the legislators decided to call this bill The Lautenberg Act. It was controversial because many big chemical companies and retailers didn't want to rock the boat and change things. Yet the Democrats persisted in trying to find enough Republican allies who might be willing to co-sponsor The Lautenberg Act and vote for a way to keep dangerous toxic chemicals out of our homes, schools, and workplaces.

According to Fred Krupp, the President of the Environmental Defense Fund, who was part of the conversations being held with Democratic and Republican legislators on how to ban chemicals that were known to be harmful or fatal, "In the midst of the negotiations over the details in the bill, I found myself talking with Senator James Inhofe, the conservative Oklahoma Republican best known in my circles for throwing a snowball on the Senate floor to mock global warming. But we didn't talk about any of that."

What the environmentalists and Democrats discovered is that Republican Senators and House members were starting to sit down at the table and offer ways to craft a bill that would pass because of two reasons:

First, they were hearing from retailers and manufacturers that there was too much "chaos" going on because each state was passing very different laws about which chemicals to ban and how much of each chemical was dangerous or not dangerous. This complicated piecemeal state-by-state approach was causing consumers to complain that they couldn't figure out which products to use and which products to avoid. Companies started spending a lot of money to reformulate products so that families and industries would be able to keep buying chemical products. Yet there were so many state-by-state inconsistencies and controversies going on, no one could figure out what was safe and what wasn't safe.

It was not only causing chaos for the chemical companies and retailers, but also cutting into their profitability. Ding, ding, ding, the magic words again, "resolving the chaos in a particular industry" in order to restore "profitability."

The second thing that caused Republican allies to emerge to move the Lautenberg Act forward was that several Democratic and Republican legislators began to have lunches, phone conversations, and meetings to spell out what different regions and states would need in order for the manufacturing and retail changes not to hurt their particular state unfairly. Both the Republican and Democratic legislators were listening carefully to one another about the chaos in the marketplace and about working toward the common goal of keeping kids and families safe from hazardous fatal chemicals. They were speaking both the language of the Democrats and the Republicans in their conversations. Senator Inhofe (the Republican from Oklahoma) led the negotiations from the Republican side and said he was extremely pleased that "these new regulations would bring greater certainty to the business community."

After the Lautenberg Act passed in 2016 and was signed into law by President Obama, Fred Krupp wrote a blog article called "This Story of Bipartisanship Will Make You Believe in Government Again." He described how, "A professor of mine at the University of Michigan Law School once said that problems become more solvable when people lower their voices and work things out. For many in Washington, even talking to the opposition, much less working across the aisle, is a sin. In an era of narrow majorities and divided government, that is a recipe for certain failure. But it appears that some are looking at the moral calculation...and realizing that if a willingness to work with people you normally oppose leads to fewer hazardous chemicals in our children's lives, we have all won."

Who are the people that you need to talk with in order to find common ground and get things done in your own corner of the world? What will it take for you and the other person to understand each other's different ways of seeing the problem and your vastly different ways of knowing when it's time to take action? Is it possible that the problems you and this person need to resolve will be much more solvable when you both lower your voices and work things out with mutual respect? I hope we will someday look back at this time of angry division and say, "Whoa. That was a tough time in our history. Thank goodness we've grown out of that rut."

Chapter Five:
WHAT'S YOUR PERSONAL JOURNEY REGARDING LGBT STRUGGLES?

A therapy client in her mid-20's named Rebecca, who is Jewish and lesbian, asked me a couple years ago, "What's the current Jewish policy on being LGBT (lesbian, gay, bisexual, or transgender)?"

I was tempted to tell her the entire history and rabbinic debates about how each of the branches of Judaism (Orthodox, Conservative, Reform, Reconstructionist, Renewal, Humanistic, and Secular) have wrestled in different ways and at different speeds with these questions during the past 45 years. It's a fascinating story. But that would have taken up far longer than her 55 minute session and I was pretty sure this lengthy history was not what she was asking from me.

So I responded to her question with a question, "What have people told you so far about how Judaism supports or doesn't support who you are?"

Rebecca smiled and replied, "That's so Jewish of you to answer a question with a question. I guess what I'm needing is some help regarding a huge disagreement my mom and my dad have been yelling at each other about for the past few years. My mom thinks it's perfectly okay for me to be out, queer, proud, and quite gender fluid at High Holidays and other Jewish events. She grew up in a very welcoming congregation and she wants me to find a congregation that is equally inclusive and supportive."

"My dad, on the other hand, grew up with extremely dogmatic parents and he's become quite alienated from all types of organized religion. He insists that Leviticus 18 is homophobia 101 and he thinks Judaism has lots of judgmental things to say about who I am."

Like most people who are trying to sort out what the Torah says and what 21ˢᵗ century rabbis have stated about sexual orientation and gender identity, Rebecca wasn't sure whether Judaism was a source of support or non-support. What would you say to her? What has been your personal experience on how Judaism deals with LGBT issues?

Sitting a few feet away from Rebecca in my office, I silently thought about the fact that with many important Jewish questions, the most accurate, short answer is usually, "Both." Think about it for a minute. If someone asks you, "Is Judaism feminist or sexist?," what's the most accurate short answer: "Both!" Or if someone asks, "Is Judaism a religion of deep faith or a religion of permissible uncertainty?," the most accurate short answer is "Both!"

Then if you ask, "Is Judaism a leading progressive force on LGBT issues or a diverse tribe that includes numerous people who are still uncomfortable with LGBT openness?" The accurate short answer is, "Both!"

Rather than characterizing Jews and Judaism as all-accepting or all-rejecting on the issues of sexual orientation and gender identity, this chapter will explore how to understand and make peace between the various conflicting opinions in your family, your community, your workplace, or your congregation. There might even be conflicting opinions that exist in your own brain and your own psyche on these issues. For example:

THE HONEST ACTIVIST. I have a longtime friend who is a hard-working executive at a major LGBT rights organization. She admitted to me recently, "I try to be open-minded about all the various expressions of gender and sexuality that I see walking into my office. But if I'm honest, I will tell you I'm not 100% comfortable with everyone and everything. I grew up with so much internalized homophobia and prejudice from my family and my schoolmates. It's hard for me to climb out of all that muddy ambivalence or to be totally comfortable when I meet someone who is way more 'fem' or way more 'butch'—or way more 'gender non-conforming' than what I grew up with in my circle of friends. In some ways I'm still trying to 'pass' or 'fit in' when I choose to wear certain conventional clothes on the days when I'm giving a speech in front of straight people I don't know well. I'm not as closeted or squeamish as I was as a teenager, but I'm nowhere as open and comfortable as my daughter's generation seems to be."

(In other words, even many LGBT activists struggle with the leftover residues of growing up in a world that has loud or soft ways of saying, "Be cautious. You're outnumbered. Keep it hidden. Don't let people know who you truly are.")

THE EVOLVING RABBI. Here's a second example of the conflicting feelings that run through our minds about LGBT issues. I remember 22 years ago when a prominent rabbi with a large following was sitting next to me at a dinner and he told me quietly, "I've been asked many times if I would be willing to officiate at a same-sex wedding under a Chuppah (a canopy for a Jewish wedding). I had to say no. I would be willing to call their event a commitment ceremony. But I'm holding out on the word 'marriage' for what I was trained to understand as the official Jewish wedding. Yet it pains me because I can see the hurt in their eyes when I have to say no."

Five years later, I spoke to this rabbi again at a conference and he told me then, "I've evolved on that particular issue. I truly wrestled with the texts and the tradition on this. After a lot of study, prayer, and conversations with colleagues that I respect a lot, my current position is that a devoted monogamous couple who sincerely wants a lifetime bond and a Chuppah, a Ketubah (a Jewish wedding contract), and the highest blessing of the community is something very Jewish, extremely sacred, and to be celebrated. I've taken some flak from some of my more traditional colleagues on this who disagree with me, but I have given this some serious thought and I see it differently than I did earlier in my career."

(In other words, even some rabbis who have one stated position on LGBT issues today are still having conversations and text-analyses that cause them sometimes to re-evaluate what their Jewish perspective will be on this issue with each passing year.)

SOME COMPLICATED QUESTIONS TO CONSIDER

Is it possible for traditional Jews and progressive Jews to get along on the questions of LGBT inclusiveness and whether to perform same-sex marriages? In the next several pages, I will describe briefly the rich history of how Jews and Judaism have dealt with the intense debates in our families and our congregations about LGBT issues.

In addition, I will be exploring what to do when there are tensions in your personal life or your work life between individuals who are comfortable with LGBT identities and those who are uncomfortable. Even in the year 2020, there are still moments when two well-meaning people say or do things that cause each other pain because of how they view LGBT topics differently.

My goal in this chapter is to offer some creative Jewish ways for dealing with the unresolved discomforts and awkward moments that still are impacting many of our family conversations, our workplace decisions, our congregational policies, and our American system of laws and rights. I'm not promising that everything will be 100% smooth or easy, but I'm hoping these creative Jewish ideas and approaches can help enormously for you and the people you care about deeply.

WHAT THE TORAH AND THE COMMENTARIES SAY

Before we get to the possible solutions, we first need to spell out one of the main reasons for the intense arguments that have caused intelligent people to take opposing sides on the issues of LGBT inclusion, whether to ordain gay and lesbian rabbis, whether to support same-sex marriage, whether to support gay and lesbian couples as adoptive parents, and how to view transgender, intersex, and gender non-conforming individuals who are seeking equal rights and protections. For many rabbis and observant Jews, it comes down to some specific lines from the Torah.

For example, in Leviticus 18 it says, "You shall not copy the practices of the land of Egypt where you dwelt, or of the land of Canaan in which I am taking you…do not lie with a male as one lies with a woman, it is an abhorrence," (or in some translations, it is a "taboo").

For many centuries, these words seemed to be saying that two men being physically intimate was not permitted (and some of the traditional commentaries and rulings extended this prohibition also to two women being physically intimate). For numerous traditional Jews today and for many fundamentalist Christians (including a sizeable number of U.S. Congressional members and judges from certain backgrounds), these words from Leviticus are seen as a non-negotiable stop sign against LGBT relationships.

But in Judaism we don't just settle for the P'shat (the surface level meaning of a line of Torah). It is our longstanding tradition as Yisra-El (which literally means the ones who wrestle and strive with the Infinite One) to wrestle carefully with each complicated line of Torah in order to see what it means on deeper levels. That means turning it over and over, as well as discussing it with a study partner, or with one another in a class or Torah service on Saturday mornings, what the particular words refer to in light of the entire Torah, along with the numerous commentaries and rulings that can guide us on how to apply those Torah words to our daily lives.

So for a moment if you want to understand this line from Torah and why some Torah-loving Jews are progressive about LGBT issues, why some Torah-loving Jews are traditional about LGBT issues, and why some are both, let's see how people have wrestled with these crucial lines from Leviticus 18.

To begin with, Jewish scholars have given us hundreds of articles and speeches that ask, "What are the practices of Egypt and Canaan that this line of Torah is referring to?" as well as dozens of articles and speeches that ask, "Why is the prohibition against homosexuality so aggressively stated by certain religious leaders, whereas the prohibitions about keeping kosher, committing adultery, and other issues are so mildly discussed?"

Each branch of Judaism has had a variety of different responses to these questions and I will attempt to describe briefly each of their viewpoints in an unbiased way so that you can decide for yourself which views you agree with and which views you don't. Here goes:

Numerous scholars in the Reform, Reconstructionist, and Renewal movements tend to view the prohibition from Leviticus 18 as possibly being about certain idol-worshipping activities that existed in Egypt and Canaan, specifically the drunken cult rituals of those cultures that we know from historical writings included prostitutes dressed up as deities and large groups of people having sex as part of what was considered at that time to be a fertility ritual. If in fact the prohibition against "lying with a man as you would with a woman" in Leviticus 18 is to warn us not to engage in orgies, idol-worshipping cult rituals, or drunken sex with prostitutes who are portraying deities, then there is a consistency in the Torah and this warning is one of several places in the Torah where the Hebrews are being urged to steer clear of the idol-worship rituals that were found in neighboring cultures.

Some Reform, Reconstructionist, and Renewal scholars also have argued that the prohibition of "don't lie with a male as you would with a woman" in Leviticus 18 was possibly written to warn Hebrews not to engage in the forced penetration, non-consensual sex that was common when a victorious army captured numerous defeated enemy combatants and treated them as slaves, often as sexual slaves after a battle. There are several places in the Torah where Hebrew followers of the One Creative Source are urged to never mistreat or force sex on anyone, even someone who has been given to you as a paid or unpaid servant after a war.

It always amazed me how compassionate the Torah is (and how far ahead of its time it was) when I was shown many years ago in a Torah discussion group the several Torah passages that describe in detail how to treat with caring and gentleness any male or female who had been assigned to you after a war to work for you. You were not allowed to be harsh or cruel to this person (even though this person had been humbled by being on the losing side of a war) because every human being has a spark of the Divine in them and you were certainly not allowed to force sex on this person (even though forced sex after a war was in those times and still is in many cultures today a common practice). So instead of seeing "do not lie with a male as you would with a woman" as a harsh attack on same-sex couples, these Reform, Reconstructionist, and Renewal scholars were asking essentially, "Is it possible to see Leviticus 18 as a compassionate warning against non-consensual sex with drunken prostitutes or with servants after a war?"

In addition, something happened in the Reform, Reconstructionist and Renewal communities after the American Psychiatric Association ruled in the early 1970's that gay, lesbian and bisexual relationships were no longer to be considered as an "illness," a "deviation," or something to be "changed." Within a few years after the scientific community began to de-stigmatize LGBT relationships, there were intense debates in the Reform, Reconstructionist, and Renewal leadership about whether to ordain gay and lesbian rabbis, and whether to support LGBT couples who wanted to make a holy, lifetime commitment to one another. It took several years and numerous argumentative debates, but these progressive branches of Judaism each voted to break free of centuries of discrimination against LGBT individuals and start being an active force in society for establishing respect and equal rights to those who love someone of the same gender and want to build a life of sacred vows and family stability with that person.

THE NEW DEBATE IN THE ORTHODOX WORLD

Many in the Orthodox branch of Judaism continue to see Leviticus 18 as an unchangeable prohibition of LGBT physical intimacy, but in the past 20 years there have been numerous voices in the Orthodox world who have wrestled with the Torah text and decided that there are complexities and a need for compassion that are equally important.

For example, Orthodox Rabbi Jonathan Sacks, the Chief Rabbi of the United Kingdom, has written that, "Compassion, sympathy, empathy, understanding—these are essential elements of Judaism. They are what homosexual Jews who care about Judaism need from us today."

Rabbi Daniel Landes, an Orthodox rabbi who has been a Torah scholar in the United States and in Israel, wrote that, "Leviticus 18 has not been erased from the Torah. But that biblical commandment does not give us license to ignore or abuse the significant number of carefully observant Jews who are LGBTQ."

Rabbi Joseph Dweck, who was the Senior Rabbi of the Spanish and Sephardic Community in the United Kingdom, taught a class on the premise that, "The entire revolution of feminism and even homosexuality in our society is a fantastic development for humanity."

Rabbi Yosef Kanefsky, an Orthodox rabbi who has led rapidly-growing congregations in Riverdale, New York and Los Angeles, California, has written that, "Homosexuality is a feature of the human condition. Recognizing the reality of sexual orientation can and should bring us to a place in which we can accept friends, children, and siblings for who they are, to grant them the dignity and respect that any person deserves, and love them as our own."

Rabbi Shmuly Yanklowitz, an Orthodox rabbi at UCLA Hillel and later at congregations in Overland Park, Kansas and Phoenix, Arizona, has written that, "As an Orthodox Jew, I believe the Bible was given by G-d, that Jewish law is binding, and that change in our religious practice cannot happen impetuously. It also means that I take the pervasive biblical call for justice very seriously. I am pro gay rights because I am an Orthodox Jew, not in spite of it."

He then went on to explain that standing up for LGBT rights and inclusion is what the overall Torah requires. Yanklowitz says we should be focusing on sexual ethics when it comes to preventing rape, making sure that our society stops objectifying women, and creating a healthy sexual ethic for monogamy and positive sexual intimacy for committed couples, rather than continuing to be obsessed with preventing gay and lesbian couples from marrying and having equal rights.

At Orthodox day schools in England, the United States, and Israel, there is now a concerted effort to prevent and stop bullying and verbal abuse against LGBT students. A British organization called KeshetUK.org has published a guidebook on how to help Orthodox schools and families from mistreating LGBT students and relatives. (Keshet is the Hebrew word for rainbow). Chief Rabbi Ephraim Mirvis, the Orthodox leader of the United Hebrew Congregations of Great Britain, wrote in the introduction to this guide (which is being replicated in several other countries), "There is an urgent need for authoritative guidance which recognizes the reality that there are LGBT students in our schools whom we have a duty to care for."

I don't know where the Orthodox branch of Judaism will be in ten or twenty years on the issues of LGBT inclusion and rights. But there has been a significant shift in tone and empathy in the past 20 years when discussing how to apply Leviticus 18 to people who are born with a deep longing to pursue a life of Jewish observance and loving relationships that are true to their nature. We'll see what happens as the next generations grow into the top levels of decision-making power.

A SERIES OF VOTES TO DECIDE A DIRECTION

One of the most intense and deeply felt debates about LGBT issues has occurred in the Conservative branch of Judaism, which attempts to honor the Torah commandments while also being sensitive to modern-day interpretations and scientific information.

In the 1980's and 1990's, the debate and the discussions within Conservative synagogues about LGBT inclusion, whether to ordain gay and lesbian rabbis, and whether to support same-sex marriage, had become quite intense. In 1992, a 15-rabbi Commission on Human Sexuality was appointed by the Conservative leadership because of a recommendation by Rabbi Elliot Dorff, the provost of the American Jewish University (which at that time was called The University of Judaism).

An expert on Jewish law, bioethics, and how to combine the wisdom of science and Torah, Rabbi Dorff cited numerous recent studies that showed why being gay or lesbian is not a "choice" or a "lifestyle," but rather a natural part of the way that approximately 10% of human beings in each era have been since the beginning of time. Dorff admitted that he is a heterosexual male who had not known much about LGBT issues until he began listening to several of his students over the years describe their personal experiences of being LGBT, Jewish, and ostracized. Dorff proposed that the Conservative movement begin to study ways to be more open to LGBT rights while at the same time honoring the Torah rules and traditions.

In his rabbinic Torah text analysis papers that he gave to the Conservative leadership, Dorff wrote that, "It is simply mind-boggling and frankly un-Jewish to think that God created 10% of humanity to have sexual drives which cannot legally be expressed! If homosexuality is an orientation over which the individual has no choice, then the proper reading of Jewish law should be that homosexual acts, like heterosexual acts, should be regulated such that some are sanctified…and others where there is coercion or lack of respect and love, perhaps even vilified."

There was substantial opposition to Dorff's recommendations. On the first round of voting, the Conservative movement's leaders turned him down and voted against any changes in the laws about LGBT rights.

But in May 1992 on the third round of voting, the Conservative Jewish leadership voted 64-50 to open up and be more inclusive and supportive of LGBT individuals.

One of the arguments that influenced some leaders of the Conservative movement was proposed by Rabbi Bradley Shavit Artson, who at that time was a congregational rabbi but later became the Dean of the American Jewish University program that trains and ordains Conservative rabbis.

Rabbi Artson did an in-depth analysis of the history of Jewish law on homosexual rights and the history of same-sex encounters during different centuries and ancient time periods. He concluded that at the time when Leviticus was written, there was no such thing as two individuals of the same gender making a lifetime commitment to be monogamous with each other and to ask for the blessing of the Jewish community for their stable and loving same-sex relationship. Artson recommended, "Since Leviticus 18 cannot possibly be outlawing something that didn't exist in reality at that time, we need to consider that it was prohibiting something other than the current situation of two people who truly love one another exclusively, are seeking to make a holy lifelong commitment, and have a deep religious desire for community support and blessing."

Artson, Dorff, and several other scholars were recommending that the Torah could still be honored and at the same time the Jewish religion could support and give its blessing to stable loving relationships between two men or between two women. Their writings are still being debated by some Jewish scholars and congregational leaders, but the shift to being support-ive of the potential holiness of LGBT love relationships had finally been approved and put into practice by the Conservative movement.

RESOLVING THE TENSIONS IN YOUR CORNER
OF THE WORLD

Now let's look at what specific instances of LGBT controversies there are in your own life currently or in the recent past. Is there a family member, friend, or work colleague who gets treated disrespectfully or talked about in a hush-hush disparaging way for being different from the majority regarding sexual orientation or gender expression? Is there a particular relative, co-worker, or fellow congregant who is uncomfortable with LGBT issues and how do you talk with this person in a compassionate way? Are there moments when hurtful or insulting remarks are said at family gatherings or at social events and you are wondering how to respond effectively?

There are some extremely useful Jewish mindfulness tools you can experiment with for dealing with these uncomfortable situations. See which of the following you've already tried and which you might want to utilize in the near future:

DISCUSSING WITHOUT SHAMING

In a heated conversation about LGBT rights, there is a Jewish method that can help preserve your friendship or family bond with someone, even if that person strongly disagrees with your point of view. It's about the tone in your voice and the way you treat the person whose views clash with your views.

Here is a quick, vivid illustration of what I mean by "tone" and "treatment":

As I mentioned earlier, Rabbi Elliot Dorff was in the minority at first when he recommended to the Conservative movement that they make a shift toward LGBT inclusion and they voted against his views twice in a row. I remember hearing about the heated debates and wondering if Rabbi Dorff was going to be able to keep his cool and his respect for others even when they were trashing him and his views in public forums and in published articles and opinion papers.

Specifically, Rabbi Dorff, a thoughtful, modest, and gentle academician originally from Milwaukee who had written several scholarly books on Jewish ethics, was facing two extremely powerful and outspoken critics of Dorff's recommendations. One was Rabbi Joel Roth, who was a sometimes-fiery leader of the Conservative movement's Committee on Jewish Law and Standards, a prominent teacher and leader at the Jewish Theological Seminary in New York, and the head of a Conservative Yeshiva in Jerusalem.

The other person aggressively criticizing Dorff's views was Dennis Prager, who stands well over six feet tall and has hundreds of thousands of loyal followers on talk radio and at his many well-attended speeches at synagogues nationwide.

Each time Dorff's views got verbally attacked by these two powerful and prominent men, I watched to see if Dorff would be able to walk the walk and not just talk the talk of "shalom bayit" (which means how to sustain a peaceful relationship with people in your home, or where you work, or in a public discourse where people strongly disagree with you).

I noticed that when addressing Dennis Prager, Rabbi Dorff spoke to Prager in the calm, caring tone of two longtime colleagues who see things very differently but who both care about Jewish continuity, ethical behavior, and human dignity. The more explosive and upset Prager got, the more calm and thoughtful Dorff became.

When addressing Rabbi Joel Roth, Dorff also had a calm, caring tone as he explained at public debates and in several writings that Rabbi Dorff and Rabbi Roth had known and respected each other for many years, that they shared the same views regarding numerous complicated moral issues and rabbinic decisions, and that they both cared deeply about each other's well-being and the well-being of their families.

As the tension built during the weeks before the third vote on whether to support LGBT rights, Dorff chose his words carefully and avoided any name-calling. He also offered a compromise solution that would embrace both the traditional Jewish laws as well as the scientific evidence and social changes that now supported the honoring of LGBT relationships.

The decision by the Conservative movement to make an official change of policy and be supportive of LGBT rights was big news worldwide and was covered by many television news shows, newspapers, and magazines.

I believe one of the reasons why Dorff eventually got the majority to vote for his policy recommendations is because Dorff and others were so inclusive and non-shaming of those who vehemently disagreed with their suggestions.

Whereas the Episcopal Christian Church in the 1990's and early 2000's has seen numerous formerly Episcopal congregations break off and refuse to associate with the central leadership after the central leadership had endorsed the ordination of LGBT priests, the Conservative Jewish movement did not split apart despite the intensity of their debates during the 1990's. Like Hillel and Shammai two thousand years ago, there was room for passionate individuals to disagree and some compromises made without the other side being talked about in a demeaning way.

How does that translate to a dinner or holiday gathering in your own family when a certain family member says something insulting or hurtful that makes you cringe? How do you keep your cool and not go off on someone who says something that you feel is truly offensive or disrespectful? How do you make a positive impact on this person and his or her repugnant statements without blowing up the family event or causing a long-lasting feud?

THE BURNING STICK OF WOOD

Here's a practical illustration of how paying attention to "tone" and "treatment" can make a significant difference in a family gathering when you're not sure what to do or say:

Several years ago my dear father, who was quite open-minded and compassionate on some issues, started talking at a holiday dinner about someone we know who is gay. My father, like many in his generation, began his comments with the words, "and the thing about faggots is…"

I felt my neck getting red and hot. My pulse started racing. I was very close to blurting out an insulting comeback line. Not only did I want to defend the gay individual who was a member of my extended family and that my dad was putting down, but I also wanted to fight back against my dad's continuing rigidity on this and certain other issues.

But then I remembered the teachings of Maimonides that I had been given many years earlier about offering reproach or feedback in a calm, private, non-shaming, one-on-one conversation that honors the sacred soul of someone with whom you disagree.

So I whispered to my dad, "Can we go into the kitchen for a minute. I want to ask you something important."

My dad looked a little nervous and hesitant. He was probably wondering if his son was going to give him a rough time about something. So my dad whispered, "Is this absolutely necessary?"

I reassured him by saying, "I promise I won't bite."

He looked at me skeptically.

I smiled and said quietly, "I promise."

Within a few seconds, the two of us walked from the dining room into the kitchen where I poured two club sodas with lime and we sat down for a brief conversation.

I began by saying, "Dad, I love you and I think of you as a very caring and kind person. So I want to offer you a dictionary definition of what the word 'faggot' means, because a lot of people don't know the origins of that word."

My dad smiled with a mischievous grin on his face, as he asked, "Is this going to be a long lecture from my son the psychologist?"

I replied, "No lecture. Just a quick dictionary definition and then you get to decide how you feel about that word."

I then explained briefly to my dad that the official definition of the words "faggot" or "fag" are "a burning stick of wood" and that it comes from the medieval European custom of the church and village leaders in a 98% Christian town rounding up homosexuals and other "heretics" for the purpose of burning them alive in the public square.

I then asked my dad, "Based on what you experienced when you were a kid in Germany, does that seem like a word you would be comfortable using again now that you know what it means?"

My dad had a serious look on his face as he responded, "I honestly didn't know."

I held his hand softly as I replied, "I truly believe you."

I never heard him use that word again.

Even though I was tempted at first to confront my dad loudly and abruptly in front of the others at that family gathering, I'm fairly certain that would have caused him to shut down or get defensive. Or if I had blurted out the first words that came into my head, which were, "I can't believe my own father is so friggin' prejudiced," I'm pretty sure that tone of voice and those words would have started a long-lasting feud between us.

What is remarkable about the Jewish approach of conversing one-on-one with respect and kindness is that the other person becomes far more likely to be able to hear what you are saying. It doesn't always work, but in the majority of situations you can help someone see the hurtfulness of certain words if you treat that person with respect and talk to them calmly in a private, one-on-one search for the truth.

HAVING THE HUMILITY TO ADMIT WE ALL HAVE SOME BAGGAGE AND DISCOMFORTS

A second Jewish tool (for dealing with hurtful words or responding to someone who is slow to accept an LGBT individual) is to get in touch with your own imperfections and your own struggles on that particular issue. Being humble in Judaism doesn't mean being weak or passive; it means admitting we all struggle at times in life and that we can have compassion for others who struggle.

For instance, before you criticize or judge someone for not being 100% comfortable about LGBT complexities, what if you took a breath and humbly recalled for a few seconds your own multi-step journey when you struggled to wade through the murky homophobic ideas and misperceptions that all of us are exposed to frequently, even in the current century.

Getting in touch with your humbleness and your humanness might include asking yourself:

- Is it possible for you to have compassion for how many months or years it took you to fully understand and accept the full diversity of gender expression and sexual orientation that exists in the world?

- Is it possible for you to have compassion and patience for someone in your family, your workplace, your congregation, or your neighborhood who is slow to appreciate and open up to the realities that you and your close friends have already accepted and affirmed?

- Are you able to appreciate that you didn't come to your current level of comfort regarding LGBT issues immediately and that others might need even longer or require more support in order to climb out of the homophobic fears and beliefs they were raised with?

Here's a real-life example of how to have humility for the fact that each of us has had some complicated baggage to sort out regarding LGBT issues and that each of us deserves some time and patience to expand beyond our prior comfort zones:

It was 1988 and I was watching on cable television the call-in show hosted by Dr. Ruth Westheimer, who at that time had several hundred thousand viewers tuning in to see her talk in scientific and compassionate ways about sexuality and intimacy. Dr. Ruth stands approximately four foot seven inches tall and speaks with a high-pitched, thick accent that includes a very unusual cackle laugh. She was born Karola Ruth Siegel in Frankfurt, Germany in 1928 in a working class Orthodox Jewish family. She lost her parents and many other relatives in the Holocaust, but Dr. Ruth never lost her incredible life force or her desire to help others.

After moving to Israel and eventually to America, she studied for many years to learn about human sexuality and how to help people improve their intimate relationships. She became famous for her radio show about healthy, responsible sexuality and then for her cable television show where she taught millions of people how to be more honest and less anxious about creating a mutually-respectful and fun sexual relationship with a beloved partner.

I still remember my wife's mom and my wife's grandmother watching Dr. Ruth with us one evening when Dr. Ruth was going on and on about "lubrication, lubrication, lubrication" and how couples needed to stop judging each other when someone simply needed some help to have adequate lubrication. For a moment (if you have some privacy) say out loud in a high-pitched German accent with a smile and a cackle laugh three times, "Lubrication, lubrication, lubrication," so you can imagine what it was like watching Dr. Ruth on national television.

My mother-in-law was laughing from head to toe. Her 90 year old mom was laughing so hard she began to choke and we had to get her some water. Dr. Ruth had clearly hit on a precious topic that both of these women knew from experience.

That same month I saw a Dr. Ruth program where a young woman called in to say she was upset about the fact that she wanted to bring her new female partner to meet her family at Passover dinner in a few weeks. The caller's mom had said no, not yet. The woman calling in to get support from Dr. Ruth wanted to make the point that her mom was being closed-minded and unsupportive by saying no to the caller's desire to have the entire family welcome her new partner at the Seder.

I had thought that Dr. Ruth would automatically side with the caller's point of view. Dr. Ruth had been a long-time supporter of LGBT rights. During the 1970's Dr. Ruth realized she knew a lot about heterosexual couples but not enough about LGBT couples, so she enrolled at the Institute for Human Identity in New York to study with a leading gay male therapist and a leading lesbian therapist about how to help couples improve their communication and their intimacy. During the AIDS crisis in the 1980's and 1990's, Dr. Ruth saved thousands of lives by being an outspoken advocate for LGBT healthcare funding and for teaching millions of people how to practice safer sex prevention methods.

But what Dr. Ruth said to this caller was surprising and it made me think. She didn't say, "Your mom is being homophobic. You are 100% right." Rather, she looked directly into the camera and spoke calmly and lovingly to this young woman caller as she explained, "I feel sorry for your mom because her daughter…that's you my sweetheart…are trying to rush her into doing something before she is ready. Your mom's already overwhelmed putting together this big family event and dealing with all the craziness of that. Now her daughter says, 'Mom, I'm lesbian, I'm bringing home my new partner for a first meeting, and I want you and the family to be 100% ready immediately on short notice to be welcoming and support-ive.' I don't think that's fair and it's not working for you and your mom. How about if you have a less public first meeting between your mom and your new partner prior to the holiday or after the holiday. That way they can get to know each other as people and not be forced to put on a show for the entire family. How about if you treat your mom as someone who needs time and patience, just like you probably needed time and patience to get fully comfortable with your sexual orientation and your truth in life. Let's be humble here and not make a pushy ultimatum that your mom can't say yes to as quickly as you wish she might. Rushing your mom or judging her for needing to slow it down a little is just going to put up a wall between you and your mom. I know you would rather have her love and her under-standing, which is much more likely to happen if you don't pressure her with an ultimatum or a rushed deadline."

After watching Dr. Ruth have so much compassion for both the young woman who wants her new partner to be welcomed by the family and for the mom who was needing a little bit of time and patience in order to make that happen, I was impressed by the humility and mutual caring that Dr. Ruth was recommending. It was not a question of who's right or who's the most open-minded. It was about two vulnerable humans slowing things down and making sure no one feels rushed or judged for being on a multi-step journey of learning to understand and appreciate one another.

As you think about someone in your life who is a little slower (or a lot slower) than you were on your road to get fully comfortable with LGBT issues, ask yourself:

Can you set aside judgment and criticism for a moment and just look into the frightened heart of this person who is saying or doing things that you wish they would stop saying or doing? Can you love (or at least be decent to) this person through these awkward steps where their fears and misconceptions seem to be louder than their ability to open up their heart fully and completely?

ONE FINAL JEWISH METHOD: FINDING THE JOY OF RADICAL AMAZEMENT FOR THE DIVERSITY OF CREATION

I will end this chapter with one additional Jewish tool for dealing with LGBT issues. It's something that has been discussed by many Jewish teachers, including Rabbi Abraham Joshua Heschel (who trained many prominent rabbis, marched with Martin Luther King, Jr. and wrote several excellent books on how to appreciate the diversity and holiness of life).

Heschel described a human spiritual phenomenon which he called opening up to "radical amazement." It might be when you look at something fascinating or beautiful in nature and you experience awe and gratitude that we live in such an abundant and diverse world. Each snowflake, each leaf, each tiny insect, each new scientific or medical breakthrough, each delicious and nutritious food or herb—we have been given so much as a result of the ongoing creation of the universe. Can we stop for a moment and just breathe in a sense of amazement, awe, or gratitude?

For some Jews, that sense of radical amazement at the rich diversity of life extends to the issue of LGBT gender expression. While many people are uncomfortable (or even hostile) toward those who live outside the two boxes of "very male" or "very female," there is an increasing awareness in our society that gender is a rich spectrum as diverse and colorful as the light spectrum of thousands of shades and hues that flashes across the sky after a rainstorm or when the sun streams in through a certain type of glass window pane or prism.

If you study Jewish sources, you will find that this amazement and appreciation for the diverse spectrum of gender expression varieties goes way back in Jewish history.

For example, most people don't realize that in the Torah, the Talmud and Mishnah commentaries there are at least six variations of gender described as part of God's creation, including:

- 149 references in Mishnah and Talmud to the Androgynous person who has both male and female characteristics.

- 181 references in Mishnah and Talmud to the Tumtum person who has indeterminate or obscured sexual characteristics.

- 80 references in Mishnah and Talmud to the Aylonit person who is identified as "female" at birth but develops "male" characteristics at puberty.

- 156 references in Mishnah and Talmud to the Saris person who is identified as "male" at birth but develops "female" characteristics later on.

In addition, there are hundreds of rabbinic and scholarly articles and written opinions about whether God is "beyond gender," "transgender," "constantly shifting in gender expression," or "male" as Adonai and "female" as Shechinah (the in-dwelling Presence).

One of the Hebrew words for God is Ha Rachaman, the Compassionate One, and it grammatically refers to the "male womb that nurtures and encompasses all of creation." What exactly is a male womb? Is it male or female, or both, or neither? If you think of the world as being nurtured and held together by a force field or a womb-like Source of support and nutrients, does it seem to you to be a male womb, a female womb, or a womb that is beyond gender?

Other scholars have written about the fact that if God is beyond gender and if we are "b'tzelem Elohim, created in the image of God," then to some extent we, too, are beyond the gender boxes of male and female. Do you see yourself and others as b'tzelem Elohim, created in the image of God? If so, does this spark of the Divine deep in your soul have a gender or is it a blend of genders, or is it beyond gender?

There are also hundreds of scholarly articles and rabbinic teachings on what is meant by the phrase in Genesis 1:27, "Then God created the first human in God's image…male and female, God created them." What was the first human exactly? Was it a gender fluid being that was both male and female? Was it a "them" rather than a "he" or a "she?"

With regard to whether we Jews are gender-compliant or gender-non-conforming on a day-to-day level, our history shows that Jews for many centuries have been in the forefront of several social change movements in which many Jewish women have said, "We are strong and can do a lot more than the typical feminine gender stereotype" and many Jewish men have said, "We can be nurturing, sensitive, compassionate, and receptive, far different from the typical male gender stereotype."

What has been your personal experience with gender stereotypes and whether they fit you or not? Have you ever rebelled against the rigid expectations that someone tried to assign to you because of your gender? Who are the Jewish role models you look to as examples of someone who took the gender roles and stretched them or discarded them in order to accomplish things that were far beyond what the "gender rules and regulations" said were permitted?

THE NEXT CIVIL RIGHTS CHALLENGE

Many people have suggested that the current discussions and arguments nationwide (about gender identity, transgender rights, bathroom access, military volunteers who are transgender, clergy who are gender non-conforming, and non-binary members of our extended families and our congregations) are today very similar to the debates and arguments that happened 30 or 40 years ago regarding gay, lesbian, and bisexual rights and protections. Which way will our society go on these issues? Will we force transgender high school students in Southern states to be forbidden from using the bathroom if it's not the one that fits this person's original birth certificate? Will we take away rights and protections from people who don't fit the two boxes of "male" or "female?" What are the various branches of Judaism doing in order to respond to these pressing issues?

So far the Reform, Reconstructionist, and Renewal branches of Judaism have issued policy declarations in 1978, 1990, 2003, 2015, and 2016 to support the rights and full equality of non-binary individuals and transgender members of the community. There are numerous rabbis, teachers, and leaders in the Reform, Reconstructionist, and Renewal communities who are out, comfortable, and accepted by many (but not all) as being beyond the two categories of "male" or "female."

The Conservative movement passed a resolution in 2016 "affirming its commitment to the full welcome, acceptance, and inclusion of people of transgender and gender non-conforming identities in Jewish life and general society." There are currently rabbinic graduates and rabbinic students in the Conservative movement who are open about their gender transitions.

The Orthodox movement currently is not officially supportive of transgender rights and protections. However, some Orthodox authorities have recognized a change in gender designation for those who have had sex reassignment surgery and the Stern College for Women at Yeshiva University in New York has had an openly transgender faculty member since 2007, the award-winning poet and literature Professor Joy Ladin, who also wrote the book "Through the Door of Life: A Jewish Journey Between Genders."

WHAT'S YOUR CURRENT LEVEL OF COMFORT?

While we don't know yet how each branch of Judaism will respond in the next several years to various transgender and non-binary issues, what we do know is that in the 21st century the search for "shalom bayit" (peaceful interactions between the diverse individuals you live with, work with, and pray with) will definitely include all of us needing to learn more about the diversity of gender expression that God or nature has created in both humans and other species. Clearly we are discovering more and more about just how diverse and unique many human beings are when it comes to gender identity. You can bet safely that in the next 10 or 20 years you will have at least one situation in your personal life or your public life where someone who is gender non-conforming or transgender will ask for your understanding, your love, and your support. How will you respond?

One reaction you might have to all this gender diversity could be, "Make it stop," or "Keep it out of my face, because I can't deal with this."

Another reaction you might have to all this gender diversity could be, "Baruch HaShem, Blessed is the Mysterious One who is beyond what we can name or describe, and who creates such diversity and beautiful variations consistently."

When you see someone in a store, at your workplace, at your synagogue, or at your dinner table who doesn't fit your expectations of how a male or a female is supposed to look or act, but rather has a gender expression or identity that is non-binary or completely unique, you get to decide how you want to treat this person.

One part of your brain, which probably prefers to fit things into predictable boxes that are either pink or blue, or male or female, will probably be uncomfortable for a few seconds or several minutes when you encounter someone who is gender fluid or gender non-conforming. Our brains often recoil a bit or put up a warning light when we see something that is new or hard to categorize.

But the spiritual part of your brain might be able to rise to the level of "radical amazement" and gratitude as you say to yourself, "Wow. This is an amazing world we live in that has such a diverse spectrum of truthful ways to be male or female or everything in between. I am grateful to be able to see and appreciate all that God has created."

"OUR TEACHER DON'T FIT ANY OF THE BOXES"

Here's an example of how different people make different choices of whether to open up or remain closed regarding gender diversity. See which of these individuals you agree with or disagree with:

Ariel is a 29 year old Jewish woman who teaches math and computer science at a Catholic school in a state I visited a few years ago for a Jewish book event where Ariel spoke with me in the meet-and-greet after the talk was over.

Assigned at birth as a male, Ariel always knew she had a female soul. At the age of 23, she began to transition to being female. Her family was accepting and supportive. Her friends were happy for her after years of seeing Ariel struggle to sort out her true identity and to finally be honest and public about it.

But at work, Ariel ran into a problem. She had been hired as a female teacher at the age of 25 based on her excellent references from her previous teaching experience at another Catholic school in a nearby city. The school administrator who hired Ariel told her in private that there were several LGBT individuals on the teaching staff and that each of them had promised to keep their personal lives secret. With mixed feelings, Ariel had agreed to follow the school policy of secrecy, yet Ariel wondered if that was even possible.

Ariel knew after almost three years at the school that her students loved her. She also knew that each of the other teachers at the school had slowly figured out that Ariel was either gender fluid or gender-nonconforming or transgender. There was a lot of gossip and rumors at the school about which teachers were lesbian, which teachers were bisexual, and which teachers had a unique gender identity. But despite the rumors and secrecy, there was an atmosphere of acceptance among most of the teachers.

Then all of a sudden at the end of Ariel's third year at that school, one of the parents of a student who was not in Ariel's classroom heard some rumors and became concerned that since Ariel had been born a male and was now supervising young women in the women's bathroom, then Ariel needed to be fired. Pretty soon Ariel's job was in jeopardy and she had to endure almost two years of intense negotiations, extremely personal conversations, and tremendous uncertainty.

As Ariel explained, "It didn't matter that I was doing extremely well as a teacher. What mattered is that this one parent was sure I was going to do something horrible in the female bathroom and needed to be let go."

Eventually the Archdiocese, the school administration, and Ariel's boss all had meetings on what to do about the concerns of this one parent. After many contentious conversations, they each decided that they didn't want to lose an excellent teacher and that Ariel had done nothing to justify being fired.

During those two years of uncertainty and negotiations, Ariel got much more involved in the Jewish community in her city than she ever had previously. She spoke with a supportive rabbi and a helpful counselor who specializes in Jewish spiritual direction and how to stay true to your purpose even when there are many obstacles in your path.

As Ariel described to me when I met her at the book event, "I think my supportive family and my Jewish sense of community really helped a lot. I know my name Ariel means 'Lion or Lioness for God,' but there were days when I felt more like a lamb than a lion."

While Ariel was glad to still have her job, the issue now for Ariel was that it was no longer possible to keep her personal life a secret. Her students asked her lots of curious questions about her gender journey, her difficult early years, and why Ariel's Jewish community was so supportive.

Ariel told me about one particular moment at her school that I will never forget. Two students from her classroom were arguing with each other during recess one afternoon about whether Ariel was "really a boy" or "really a girl." As Ariel tells it:

"The first student made a well-reasoned argument on the playground that if someone is born with one gender it is always a part of who that person is. The other student made a well-reasoned argument on the playground that if someone knows inside that a specific other gender is closer to the truth, then just that new gender identity should be honored by everyone who cares about that person."

Ariel continues, "But then suddenly a third student entered the conversation and announced, 'Hey, cut it out! No more arguing. Our teacher don't fit any of the boxes. Ariel is Ariel and in my opinion Ariel is awesome and unique and amazing. I'm grateful to God every day that I have a teacher who is this smart and caring."

In terms of Jewish tools for peace making, this third student from Ariel's class is a vivid example of Rabbi Abraham Joshua Heschel's concept of "radical amazement." It's unlikely that this Catholic school child had read or heard of Heschel. But in her description of feeling grateful to God every day for something unique and awesome, she was spontaneously rising above the labels and categories that cause people to argue or clash. Instead, she was thanking the Infinite Source of the Universe for creating such uniqueness and such diversity.

What would it be like if in 2020 (and beyond) we could feel awe and gratitude for the uniqueness of each person we meet, rather than trying to put that person into a box or category (and then getting upset if that person simply doesn't fit any of the restrictive boxes)? Is that something you have already experienced—feeling wonder and amazement at the diversity of human individuality? Or is it something you would like to consider the next time you are face to face with someone who is quite different and unique?

Chapter Six:

WHAT HAPPENS WHEN YOU DISAGREE ABOUT RELIGIOUS DECISIONS AND HOLIDAY GATHERINGS

The couple in my office on a Thursday afternoon has been arguing for almost a half hour (and for several days at home). Their clashing viewpoints are about what to do regarding their 12 year old son Henry who was refusing to study each week for his bar mitzvah, which was coming up in less than six months. The clock was ticking and their strong-willed son had not yet begun to prepare for his Torah reading, his service project, or his speech.

The dad was visibly upset as he argued, "We've got to stop coddling him. I think it's time we took away Henry's cell phone until he starts being more cooperative and motivated."

The mom argued back, "You're being rigid like your dad used to be when you were a kid. Henry needs his cell phone to have a social life and we need him to have his phone with him because that's how we know where he is and if he's safe."

Instead, the mom suggested, "He just needs a reason to stop digging in his heels and start making the six months of preparations more enjoyable. Maybe what he needs is the enticement of a two-day visit to Disneyland next month if he starts doing one hour a day of practicing his Torah chanting and the other parts of the prayer service he will be leading. He needs to feel like this is a pleasurable thing, rather than a drudge or a punishment."

The dad rolled his eyes and commented, "That is way too soft and it makes us look like pushovers. He's been acting like a slacker for the past three months and there isn't much time left."

As their argument became more intense with each passing minute, I began to wonder if the two parents were not only disagreeing about how to motivate their son, but also about their differing feelings about the bar mitzvah itself. Like many families when there are clashes over how to deal with opposing ideas regarding wedding details, a bris or baby naming, a bar or bat mitzvah, or other Jewish life cycle decisions, the issue is often not just about family dynamics but also about significant spiritual and religious disagreements.

So I opened up the conversation and asked these two parents, "What do the two of you feel is important about your son's upcoming bar mitzvah and how does your son feel about the idea of a bar mitzvah?"

Their answers were worlds apart. For the dad, "A bar mitzvah is something I was forced to do when I was 13 and I resented it at the time, but later was glad I did it. For me, it's just something you do because it's important to your parents, your grandparents, and the continuity of the Jewish people. Even if it doesn't make sense at the time when you're turning 13, or if the kid thinks it's mostly about having a fancy party, later on the kid realizes this was something that means a lot to so many people in the family and it's not right to let your family members down. It's like learning to go to work even on the days when you feel like staying home. It's part of becoming a mature human being with responsibilities."

For the mom, it was quite different. She had grown up wanting to have a bat mitzvah, but her parents had felt it was very important for sons and less important for daughters to have a coming-of-age ritual at age 13. So they told her to wait until her Sweet 16 and she always felt a bit sad that many of her friends had a bat mitzvah and she had missed out. She spoke softly with a few tears in her eyes as she said, "I want our son to experience the holy moment of leading the congregation in prayer and being seen for the first time as a responsible member of the community who can speak from the heart about a chapter of the Torah and inspire people with thoughtful insights on what it means to him personally."

I thanked both the dad and the mom for their equally valid ideas about the reasons for a bar mitzvah, which caused them to calm down and stop arguing for a few seconds. But the tensions flared up again a minute later when they began to talk about the son's perspective and they quickly realized they had completely different ideas about what their son's ideas were regarding the bar mitzvah itself.

The dad was sure that their son Henry "couldn't care less about anything religious or spiritual." The mom disagreed and argued that, "Henry happens to be quite spiritual and deep in his own unique way. He loves being out in nature and he's extremely adamant about environmental issues and saving the planet."

The dad replied, "What the heck does nature and environmentalism have to do with a bar mitzvah?"

The mom responded, "It has everything to do with it. A bar mitzvah is about taking responsibility for being a mature, caring person who wants to protect and sustain God's fragile creations which are under attack right now. Our son has that kind of caring and a deep sense of stewardship in his soul if we find a way to encourage it."

The dad looked exasperated as he commented, "That's a load of bull. I think Henry's just being a rebellious teenager. There are millions of kids who have studied hard for a bar mitzvah. Our son simply needs to realize it's part of growing up."

Does this disagreement about a Jewish event sound like anything you've experienced in your own family or your congregation? Is there ever an argument or a power struggle over whose way is going to prevail (and who is going to be ignored or trampled over)?

When it comes to how to do Passover, Chanukah, High Holidays, Shabbat, or life cycle events like a bar or bat mitzvah, is there ever a debate between those who say, "You do it because it's something you just do, it's a tradition," versus those who say, "Wait a minute, we're only going to do this if it makes sense to us personally and if we can find some joy and meaning in it."

Are there ever moments when you feel discouraged or say silently, "Why are we arguing again about the intricacies of being Jewish? Why can't we talk about these important issues without becoming all bent out of shape?"

GOING CREATIVE AND FINDING A SPARK

I've found as a therapist that when family members or romantic partners get into a debate about whose way of practicing a particular tradition or ritual is "the only way," it drives people apart. My job as a therapist is not to tell people what to believe or how to practice their religious beliefs (or lack of beliefs), but rather to brainstorm with them on ways of respecting and including each other's differing beliefs that too often get ignored or overlooked. My goal is to make sure each family member or partner in a relationship has a chance to be heard without being mocked, as well as feeling included and treated fairly whenever religious or spiritual decisions are being made in their own family or their primary relationship.

With the two parents of the 12 year old son who hadn't been preparing yet for his upcoming bar mitzvah, that mutually respectful brainstorming process began in my office when I asked them to read carefully a few photocopied sentences and to explore, "Is there something in your son's Torah portion that he might connect with or be inspired about in a personal or meaningful way?"

It happened that Henry's Torah portion for the week of his bar mitzvah was going to be "Va-yetzei" (Genesis 28:10-Genesis 32), which is where our ancestor Jacob leaves home to start his adult life. According to that particular Torah portion, Jacob has a fascinating and memorable middle-of-the night experience in which he sleeps under the stars with a stone under his head and he has a dream about envisioning God's Presence and being given a holy purpose and a positive direction for the future.

After the two parents finished reading those lines together as partners, the dad commented, "I don't know if our son is going to connect with any of this. It's definitely interesting to me as an adult, but I worry that Henry is far more focused on his computer games and his slacker friends who come from families that have a lot more money than we do and these parents let their kids get away with much too much. I doubt that any of them are exploring the deeper spiritual meaning of a Torah passage."

But the mom had something very practical to say after reading the brief Jacob dream passage with her husband. She suggested to her spouse, "I've got a crazy idea, honey. Are you ready for something unusual that might possibly help Henry to be motivated and personally interested in his bar mitzvah preparation process?"

The dad leaned forward in his chair and smiled, "I'll try anything if it's going to work. Maybe it's time for something a little crazy."

Then the mom took her husband's hand in her hand and said, "I think our son Henry responds best when he gets to feel something with all five of his senses, rather than just with the conceptual part of his brain. He might enjoy having a genuine sensory experience of what it was like for Jacob to be out in the wilderness, away from the familiarity and comforts of his family home, and having some clues emerge about his future. If we rent some camping equipment and we do an overnight at one of the state parks, or maybe at one of the campgrounds near the ocean, I'll bet we could re-enact the story of Jacob's leaving home, sleeping under the stars, and having a vision of his purpose in life that shook him to his core."

The dad replied, "I didn't know you liked camping out."

The mom laughed, "If it means our son having a positive vision for his future, I'm absolutely a camper."

The dad thought for a moment and said, "What if he doesn't want to do this. For me it would be kinda nerdy to be out on an overnight with my mom and my dad."

The mom suggested, "How about it we invite Henry's best friend Dylan who has done a lot of camping with his parents and his older brother."

The dad replied, "That might make it easier for Henry to say yes and to get into it. I've always wanted to take the family on a camping vacation where we could get away from all our electronics."

The couples' counselor part of me was very happy at that moment. I didn't know what would happen next when the two parents offered this unusual idea to their son or if the overnight under the stars was going to change Henry's lack of motivation about the bar mitzvah. But I was glad to see Henry's parents working as teammates and being creative together.

THE SEARCH FOR AUTHENTIC MEMORABLE MOMENTS

As it turned out, that cooperative brainstorming conversation in my office was the beginning of something unexpected for this family. The husband and wife went home and found out that Henry was somewhat open to the idea of an overnight under the vast sky with Henry's friend Dylan along to be the expert guide on how to set up their campsite and deal with all the challenges of being away from their usual comforts. Instead of just memorizing the Torah portion for chanting it at the bar mitzvah ceremony in a little more than five months, Henry said he might be willing to re-enact the Jacob dream story and see if being in nature inspired anything for him personally. So the planning for a camping experience and the equipment rental were given a tentative "Yes" from Henry.

A few days after their night under the stars, I saw the two parents in my office and I asked, "How was it?"

The dad told me, "Well, there were some nasty flying bugs and none of us slept very well. But something did happen for our son Henry when we re-enacted the steps of putting a stone under our heads, looking up at the sky, and being out in nature away from all of our usual distractions. I'll let my wife tell you because Henry confided in her long after midnight out by the campfire when I eventually drifted off to sleep."

The mom then described the two conversations she had with her son Henry during and after the overnight camping experience. She said, "I guess in our family there are at least three different ways to be Jewish. My husband is someone who says the rules are the rules and you do what the tradition says. My way has always been to find a personal emotional connection to the holiday or the life cycle event and then to enjoy the deep moments I get from these religious experiences."

The mom then smiled with pride as she explained, "I'm starting to have a glimpse into what might be Henry's way of being Jewish. Camping out in nature gave Henry and me a chance to talk in ways we've never really talked before. Essentially, Henry told me at around three in the morning that his way to deal with the mysteries of life is to be curious and question, but not to be completely convinced on whether there is a God or whether there is a correct way to do a ritual. Henry admitted to me that he did feel some sort of vague Presence hovering around us and between us on that night under the stars and that he often feels connected to something bigger and mysterious when he's taking a walk in nature or helping out in our garden. But Henry's not sure what to call that vague Presence and he doesn't like anyone telling him what to call it."

Then the dad spoke and added, "So in the late morning when we were driving home, Henry asked if it would be ok at his bar mitzvah ceremony for him to be honest about how he viewed the Jacob dream story. Henry said he felt somewhat similar to Jacob having an experience of a mysterious source of insights and a sense of wonder when he was out in nature under the stars. But Henry wanted to know if we would be mad at him if he admitted he wasn't sure what to call that Presence or whether he is completely a believer at this point in his life."

The dad continued, "I told him I was 100% supportive that Henry gets to speak with honesty at his own bar mitzvah and to let people know what he experienced and what he's not yet ready to sign up for in terms of permanent faith or certainty. I told him I think it's very Jewish to be able to be honest and authentic about this stuff, to ask questions, and to keep searching. At that moment, I turned to look at Henry and saw a smile on his face. It's like he finally had found permission to be genuine and interested in his own personal way to become a bar mitzvah."

LISTENING TO EACH PERSON'S DIFFERENT WAYS OF DESCRIBING THE INDESCRIBABLE

While I can't guarantee that every family with a reluctant family member will have as quick or profound a breakthrough as happened for Henry and his parents, I will say that the key element from their experience is something you can utilize with your own loved ones.

I believe they were successful as a family during the final five months leading up to their son's bar mitzvah because they had begun to listen caringly and were willing to respect the different "spiritual languages" that each of them spoke. The dad felt respected by his wife and son for how much he valued the traditions and the rules of how to do things. The mom felt respected by her husband and son for how they were creating together some meaningful experiences and deeper connections. The son felt respected by both of his parents that they were allowing him to question and be honest about his insights rather than having to pretend to be more certain or more traditional than he was at that moment.

In your own family or in the congregation where you attend services often or rarely, is it possible that some of the disagreements and clashes could be reduced or resolved somewhat if each individual began to listen caringly (without mocking or trampling) to the different feelings and different spiritual styles of the various participants. For example:

- Can you be patient and respectful to those in your family or your congregation who are focused on the rules, the obligations, the steady habit-building, and the commitments, as they seem to say, "We need to do it this particular way because that's the way it's traditionally been done."

- Can you be patient and respectful to those in your family or your congregation who feel the need to search for deeper meanings and experiential moments in order to connect with a holiday, a ritual, or a traditional practice, as they seem to say, "Let's see how to make it come alive first and then we'll decide if we're going to include that song, that prayer, that interpretation, or that ritual in the choices of various things we will be doing at that upcoming event."

- Can you be patient and respectful to those in your family or your congregation who are skeptical or unsure about God or religion, but who still have moments in life when they are curious, passionate, or exploratory about the mysteries of life and how science, nature, art, music, history, or culture help them address those mysteries. Can you stop arguing about theology and faith for a moment, and instead start building together some creative ways of combining science and spirituality, nature and Torah text, individualism and community.

One of the things I love about Judaism is that our religion is often remarkably open to each individual having a personal way of connecting with the unexplainable and the indescribable mysteries of life. If unfortunately, no one mentioned this "openness to differing opinions" to you in the family or congregation where you grew up, please consider the fact that there are at least three and possibly more than a hundred different examples from Jewish teachings about why it's "very Jewish" to have different ways of viewing a spiritual or religious discussion.

Here are a few quick illustrations to help you get the sense of how Judaism encourages diverse opinions and perspectives:

THE STANDING PRAYER. There is an extremely important traditional prayer called the Amidah (the standing prayer or the great prayer) that gets recited prominently at Shabbat services and daily services. It begins with the words "Blessed are You, the God of Abraham, the God of Isaac, the God of Jacob, (and in many egalitarian congregations) the God of Sarah, the God of Rebecca, the God of Rachel, and the God of Leah…"

To an English major or a grammarian, it seems terribly incorrect to be saying "the God of" so many times in one sentence rather than the simpler and more grammatically accurate "God of Abraham, Isaac, Jacob, Sarah, Rebecca, Rachel, and Leah."

Many Jewish scholars have weighed in on this question as to "why does this crucial prayer have an additional 'and the God of' phrase for each of these different individuals?" The answer most scholars have offered is that, "In Judaism each individual has a somewhat different experience or relationship with the One Infinite Source. So in the Amidah prayer we don't assume we all have the same beliefs and experiences, but rather we honor that each of our ancestors and each Jew today has their own unique ideas and connections to the One Creative Source that is beyond what any of us can fully describe and we cannot expect another person to have the exact same sense of God that we do.

THE KADDISH PRAYER. A similar theological concept is found in the well-known Kaddish prayer that most people associate with honoring the memory of a loved one and it is also recited at the end of each sub-section of the prayer service on Saturday mornings and on weekdays. Many scholars have asked, "Why does the Kaddish prayer (which celebrates the exquisiteness and preciousness of life even during a time of mourning) have a fascinating sentence that describes God as 'the One who is beyond any blessing and song, any praise and consolation that are uttered in this world.'"

Some scholars have suggested that this is a clear statement that in Judaism we humbly admit we can't quite describe what God is and we are forever searching, wrestling, exploring, receiving, and transmitting clues as to God's attributes and impact on our lives, but we can't possibly know the big picture for sure.

As one scholar explained in describing how the Kaddish prayer works, "In a Saturday morning prayer service each sub-section of the service has these majestic songs and profound prayers trying to connect with the indescribable Presence that surrounds us, connects us, and inspires us. But at the end of each sub-section we stop for a moment, say the Kaddish prayer, and humbly admit that the One we are singing to and praising is still way more than we can ever imagine with our limited human brains and our limited human words and melodies. We remind ourselves not to get arrogant and think 'we have figured out God once and for all time,' so that we can continually be in awe that whatever we imagine God to be, we are probably only touching a tiny part of what we are still learning and discovering about how this connected universe operates or how it was created. The specific line we say often in the Kaddish prayer is to alert us that God and God's mysterious ways are beyond all that we humans can analyze, sing, say, or describe."

THE PASSOVER FOUR CHILDREN. There is also a fascinating short teaching in the middle of almost every traditional or progressive Passover Seder that describes (with some variations depending on which Hagadah you have this year) that there are four types of children and their different ways of responding to the Hagadah story of the Exodus.

One child is very knowledgeable and needs to be talked to with detailed information and insights. One child is quite simple or uninformed and needs to be talked to with gentle easy-to-understand clues about the meaning of the Passover story. Another child is quite removed and distant, not even sure how or what to ask, saying only, "What does any of this have to do with me," to which the group is encouraged to welcome and support this child who feels distant, removed, and unsure. Finally, there is the rebellious child who feels somewhat defiant or in opposition to what is being described at the Seder and it's suggested that this child needs to be welcomed and honored as well, especially since the Passover story is about rebellious midwives and defiant courageous Hebrew slaves who are taking risks to walk through wild waters and strive for freedom.

This short teaching about the four types of children (or the four personality types of what we still tend to be like as adults as well) says that the group at the holiday gathering needs to welcome and include all four of these personality types (or inner traits that we all have to some extent). It doesn't say banish, ignore, or beat this personality trait into submission.

What a radical and compassionate teaching this is in nearly every Passover Hagadah. It says to honor and to welcome each of the different attitudes, opinions, and personality types in your family or your congregation, even if those views are somewhat uncomfortable for you. It urges us to treat each person (even those we find a bit irritating) with kindness and inclusion.

Maybe this repeated emphasis in Judaism on inclusion and caring comes from the numerous Torah and Passover phrases that say, "You need to be patient and kind with the stranger, because you were once a stranger." (Some say the Torah mentions at least 36 times to be good to the stranger in your midst).

Or this repeated emphasis in Judaism on inclusion and kindness might be because we are being asked to emulate the deep caring of a compassionate and generous Source that is continually creating and expressing even when the human partners are distracted, hesitant, or defiant.

Regardless of where it comes from, there is definitely a strong and persistent emphasis in Judaism on opening your heart to the person who says contrary ideas that show he or she has a different set of clues about the universe than the ones you tend to focus on. Can you take a breath and be gentle with this person, especially if it might result in making your next family gathering or your next congregational event less contentious and more peaceful?

A FEW MORE WAYS TO GET CREATIVE SO THAT NONE OF YOUR GUESTS FEEL SLIGHTED

When there are religious differences in your extended family or your circle of friends, you might find that planning and hosting a successful holiday get-together sometimes requires the wisdom of Solomon and the patience of Job to prevent or resolve clashes or hurt feelings.

In some families, the fact that one guest is very religious and another guest is very secular might seem at first to be an irreconcilable problem. But if you think it through ahead of time with some creativity and compassion, you might be able to come up with some innovative solutions for hosting this diverse group without anyone feeling slighted.

For example, if you are inviting a group to your home for Shabbat, Chanukah, Passover, or some other event, you might be faced with the question of how to make sure those who are kosher, those who are vegan, and those who are allergic to certain foods all can celebrate together in peace.

I've explored this issue with numerous people in my counseling practice and my personal life. The best solution I've ever heard came from a counseling client of mine who told me, "My husband and I are strongly Jewish but we don't keep kosher. Yet when I invite for a holiday or Shabbat gathering certain family members and friends who keep kosher, or who have food allergies, or a vegan diet, I make sure to find the exact foods and the correct preparation steps so that my guests won't feel slighted or unable to attend. My spouse thinks I'm nuts to be so careful and considerate, but for me it's more important to make someone feel welcome and respected than to try to do what's easy or quick."

This counseling client added, "I used to view the kosher rules and the vegan rules as being a burden, but now I see them as a chance to practice mindfulness and human decency, to pay attention to each specific ingredient and the impact it might have on someone I care about. It's how I would want someone to treat me and my family—to stretch a little and make it possible for us to celebrate the holiday together as a cohesive group that honors and includes all our diverse ways. Last month for a Shabbat dinner at our home, I found some recipes for a vegan lentil-walnut fake chopped liver and a non-dairy lasagna with gluten free noodles. Everyone loved what I made and I felt like I'd brought us together in such a fun way."

Has that ever happened for you when you were hosting or being a guest at a holiday dinner? Did someone treat you with extra kindness so that you or a loved one wouldn't feel slighted or disregarded? Did you ever go the extra mile to make sure one of your guests felt included rather than inconvenienced or mistreated? I once heard a friend say that the mark of a good host or hostess is someone who causes each guest to be able to say, "I felt at home and very taken care of—maybe even more so than how it is in my own family of origin."

THE DISCUSSION QUESTIONS THAT PUT EVERYONE ON AN EQUAL FOOTING

Another creative method to make a Shabbat or holiday gathering come alive in an inclusive, peaceful way is to have a discussion question in the middle of the evening that doesn't turn into a power struggle over who knows more or who has "the only right answer." Rather, it can be a wonderful group bonding experience if you offer a discussion question that causes each person to open their hearts and get to know each other on a deeper level without any one person being the bigshot, the expert, or the dominator.

For example, at a Shabbat dinner it's easy to ask each guest to speak for 1 minute maximum on "What is one small moment or large moment that you are grateful about this week." You can tell your guests it's ok to pass or to say something big or small that gives you a sense of thankfulness or perspective. Even on a very stressful week, there can still be some moments you look to with gratitude and appreciation. Since everyone can answer this question and no one's personal answer is right or wrong, it allows each of your guests to be included as equals.

Or at Chanukah, a question that can allow each guest to be on equal footing could be something like, "In two minutes or less, what is a time in your life when you were unlike the majority and you stood up for how you were different?"

Or at Passover, a question that can inspire and connect all of your guests as equal participants might be, "Like Nachshon in the Exodus story who walks into the turbulent Sea of Reeds before he knows for sure if he will be ok and make it through safely, what is a time in your life when you took a step forward in spite of all the fears or hesitations and it turned out well."

Or in a Sukkah dinner gathering, each person can be on equal footing if the discussion question is, "In two minutes or less, who is someone in your life past or present whose good attributes, caring, or mentorship made an impact on you and you would like to invite that person's Neshama or soul into the Sukkah as one of the Ushpizin (the invited holy ancestors or recent role models)."

I can't guarantee that your guests will never fall into the awkward habit of talking too long or acting like an arrogant expert. But if you start by proposing a creative discussion question that allows each guest to shine equally and then if you bring out a talking stick or a cell phone timer to make sure only one person at a time speaks and for only a minute or two each, it usually goes extremely well.

I've found in my own life on numerous occasions that a group of people who didn't know each other when they first arrived did start to feel like long-time friends by the end of the evening because of how these discussion questions at holiday and Shabbat gatherings cause each person to speak from the heart and to say something deep, profound, and genuine.

Sometimes it helps if you or someone you trust goes first to model that it's ok to say something genuine and sincere in answer to these questions, so that others will also follow with personal and insightful answers that cause each member of the holiday gathering to think, reflect, and feel a part of something creative and holy. As the host or hostess for a holiday gathering, you get to set the tone. Will it be inclusive and connecting, or will it be a competition between one or two dominators that causes the others to feel one-down or invisible? The way you greet each new person and the way you set up the discussion part of the evening will make a huge difference on whether the group feels a sense of holiness or a sense of discomfort.

THE PRO-ACTIVE STEPS FOR YOUR MOST VOLATILE GUESTS

There is one other thing you can do to increase the likelihood of peaceful, warm interactions and fewer headaches at an upcoming holiday evening or life cycle event. You can have a pro-active phone call or lunch ahead of time with the one or two family members, colleagues, or congregants who are most likely to start a clash or an intense verbal battle at your next sacred gathering.

Here's what that pro-active phone call or lunch might entail:

- Decide ahead of time if there are one, two, or several people who tend to get upset, contentious, or verbally assaultive at holiday gatherings or life cycle events.

- Set up a phone call or lunch with each person individually at least a week prior to the holiday event.

- Ask this sometimes-volatile person calmly and respectfully to let you know how you can be supportive so that this individual will have a good experience at the upcoming event. You might want to say, "I'm calling several people ahead of time to make sure that everyone will feel comfortable and respected at the upcoming holiday dinner. Is there anything I should know ahead of time on how to make this a good event for you and your loved ones?"

• The goal of this phone call is not to criticize or rehash what awkward or explosive moments there were in the past. It's rather to make sure this person feels included, respected, and treated with kindness so that he or she doesn't walk in with a chip on the shoulder and a likelihood of going off at the slightest provocation.

• You might want to find out if there are any clashes, misunderstandings, or power struggles brewing as you approach the next holiday or special event. This will give you a chance to do some good listening and peacemaking with all the individuals who are a little edgy a week prior to the family gathering.

• Rather than seeing this as a huge burden or an unnecessary irritation, you might want to consider the fact that nearly every family and every organization has a few kinks to work out whenever there is going to be an important meeting or a joyful celebration. We humans have lots of emotional baggage we carry around and it is very normal and smart to be able to lighten and resolve some of that baggage either days or weeks before each of your guests walk through your door.

• Once you have calmly listened to whatever this sometimes-volatile person has on his or her mind a week or two prior to your holiday gathering, feel free to ask this person an important question in a caring and non-judgmental tone of voice that says, "Can I ask for something from you at this upcoming holiday dinner (or wedding or bar/bat mitzvah)? I've put a lot of time and energy into making it a pleasant event for everyone who is going to be there. I know that you and _____ have some issues and some history with each other. Is there a chance you can help me out and not get into a clash with _____ at this next event, even if _____ says or does something you don't like? Can I count on you to do whatever you can to keep the peace no matter what anyone says or does?"

In most cases, the sometimes-volatile family member or colleague will feel cared about and appreciated that you are truly listening to his or her point of view, that you are reaching out and asking for help, and that you are talking in such a caring and respectful way. While there still might be some volatile individuals who simply can't control themselves or who will refuse to promise ahead of time to be civil, at least you will have given this person something to think about and to know that you are watching him or her closely in the hope that this person will do much better this time than last time.

For some extra insurance, it often helps to ask ahead of time for the assistance of at least one or two family members who have some clout or some good rapport with this sometimes-volatile individual. You can look for someone who has the ability to give some strong, quiet, "don't go there" eye contact with the sometimes-volatile individual if things start to get intense at the upcoming family holiday event. Or someone who can take the volatile person for a walk or a supportive cooling off conversation in a side room if an explosive argument starts to happen.

Several years ago my wife Linda and I were hosting a somewhat large gathering at our home for one of the Jewish holidays and I knew that one of my cousins is married to a guy who loves to start heated arguments and say hurtful, condescending things. He's a very intelligent guy and can be quite kind and empathic at times. I was sad when I learned that he was raised by an extremely demanding dad who had a similar "rip them to shreds" approach to family disagreements and intense conversations. Apparently there was a lot of anger, one-upmanship, and verbal harshness in this guy's formative years. I had seen this highly-intelligent individual get upset and blow up at people at other events in the past and I was hoping he wouldn't have a similar explosion at the gathering that we were putting together for an upcoming holiday.

So I did two things a couple of weeks before the holiday dinner. First, I had a long relaxed check-in phone call with the sometimes-explosive guy to see how he's doing, to find out if he's willing to do everything in his power to have the upcoming event go smoothly, and to ask in a calm, respectful way for "his personal help and suggestions on what we could do as family members to make sure the religious or political conversations at the holiday dinner didn't turn into a shouting match or an ugly scene."

When I finished my short gentle request, I waited for him to reply and there was silence for several seconds on the phone. Then he asked, "Are you saying that you're worried I'm gonna make a scene like what happened the last time?"

I responded playfully, "On a scale of one to ten, I'd say I'm about six worried. I'm also hoping the evening will go well and I'm asking several people for their help to make that happen. Can I count on you to do whatever you are able to do to keep things peaceful if there are some intense conversations?"

I heard him laugh and then he said, "You don't need to worry. I'll be good."

Then I took the extra insurance step and had a check-in, "how are you doing" phone call with this guy's older sister who was also going to be at the holiday dinner. I made sure not to say anything negative or gossipy about her younger brother or to rehash what happened at some of the previous holiday dinners.

I simply talked with her about her career and what dish she wanted to bring to the pot luck gathering. Then I mentioned to her near the end of our phone call, "Can I ask for your help about something?"

She replied, "Of course. I'll do anything to help out."

I explained, "At the upcoming holiday dinner, there might be some religious or political disagreements and that's fine with us. But if you notice anyone starting to heat up or if it begins to sound like personal attacks or one-upmanship, would you be willing to put your hand on that person's knee or take that person for a short walk so that the conversation can remain respectful even when people disagree with each other?"

The older sister laughed and said, "You mean will I be the Holiday Whisperer for my beloved little brother? Of course I'd be willing to do that. I love him and I want it to be a good evening for him and for everyone else."

The night of the holiday gathering, a discussion did start up about some specific religious differences between this volatile guy and one of the other guests. After a few seconds, it started to become a little bit heated and adversarial. I made sure to have some calm, reassuring eye contact with the explosive guy as if to say, "Hey dude, I hope you will keep the promise you made to me on the phone."

I also saw that the older sister put her hand gently on his knee under the table to remind him lovingly, "Keep it together, little brother. Let's not repeat what happened last time."

As a result of these two pro-active steps, we managed to have a healthy and mutually-respectful discussion at that dinner gathering about some important religious issues and the differing points of view that had come together peacefully in our dining room. Yes, there were some passionate feelings and opinions. But there was also civility, humor, patience, and the chance for each person's experience and insights to be expressed without name calling, hurtful words, or snarky comments.

After the guests went home, I called this guy on his cell phone to thank him personally for how he contributed to the success of the evening. I said, "I'm glad that in this family we can have very different ways of practicing religion and yet we're able to do holidays together in peace. Thank you for helping to make that a reality."

He quickly responded in an almost dismissive way, "Not a problem. I wasn't worried."

After a few seconds of quiet on the phone, he added one more thing in a soft, almost-vulnerable voice. He said, "Thanks for inviting me even after how I was at the previous event. It meant a lot to me and my family because we've been excluded from some other places in recent years. It's not easy being the way I am sometimes."

Productive and mutually-respectful conversations between people who see things very differently sometimes takes a little extra planning and teamwork. But it's definitely worth the extra effort.

I hope this book and the mindfulness methods in each chapter can help you and your loved ones and colleagues to achieve these precious moments of peace and healing between people who have clashed intensely in the past.

You've probably noticed in your own life and your extended circle of acquaintances that we are living in a strange time when harshness and divisiveness have become extremely widespread. Our world, our families, and our congregations need courageous individuals and successful methods to reverse that trend.

I invite you to share these methods and examples with others that you know personally and I pray that you will be part of an equally widespread effort toward changing the way that people talk with each other about religion, politics, personal values, and how to respect diversity. We know as Jews what happens when meanness and closed-mindedness begin to dominate. Please do all that you can to make sure that we turn this around while there is still time.

NOTES AND SOURCES

CHAPTER ONE:
"Maimonides and others recommend three crucial steps…"
See "Maimonides Reader," edited by Isadore Twersky, (New York: Behrman House, 1972), pp. 434-5, and "Maimonides, Mishneh Torah, Hilchot Dei-ot, 6:7, and Estelle Frankel, "The Art of Giving and Receiving Honest Feedback or Rebuke," The Forward, November 10, 2016.
"Mahlbeen has several meanings…"
See "The Ten Challenges," by Leonard Felder, (New York: Harmony/Crown, 1997), p. 130-1.
"Making someone ashamed is like shedding blood…"
See Baba Metzia 58b and in the Stone Edition Chumash, (Brooklyn: Mesorah, 1993), p. 411.
"Rabbi Nathan in the Talmud…"
Found in Baba Metzia 59b.
"Rabbi Miriam Hamrell's weekly discussion group on Mussar…"
For more information, see www.AhavatTorahLA.org

CHAPTER TWO:
"Al Franken allegedly said…"
See Samantha Cooney, "All the Women Who Have Accused Al Franken of Sexual Misconduct," Time Magazine, December 7, 2017.
"Long articles in The New York Times and The Atlantic…"

See "Al Franken Has Regrets, Kirsten Gillibrand Does Not," New York Times, July 23, 2019, and Emily Yoffe, "Democrats Need to Learn from Their Al Franken Mistake," The Atlantic, March 26, 2019.

"News reports that said major donors…"
See Amanda Terkel, "Kirsten Gillibrand Pays the Price for Speaking Out Against Al Franken," HuffPost, August 1, 2018.

"Senator Gillibrand was asked by an interviewer…"
See Chris Hayes, MSNBC Town Hall Live, March 18, 2019.

"Rabbi Isaac two thousand years ago suggested…"
Found in Babylonian Talmud, Kiddushin 80b and in Joseph Telushkin, "Jewish Wisdom," (New York: Morrow, 1994), p. 132.

"The Baal Shem Tov said about sexual thoughts…"
See David Biale, "Eros and the Jews," (Berkeley: UCalif Press, 1997), p. 132, and Rodger Kamenetz, "The Jew in the Lotus," (New York: Harper Collins, 1994), p. 126, which is based on the Talmudic passage from TB Abodah Zarah, 20a.

CHAPTER THREE
"In the previous week's portion Sarah and Hagar…"
See Genesis 16: 1-16.

"The plot begins to twist…"
See Genesis 16: 4-5

"The current week's Torah portion Va-yeira…"
See Genesis 21: 1-21

"In 2018 there was a 6 part series…"
January 14, 2018 to August 12, 2018, "A Study Hall for Seekers" one Sunday afternoon per month at Ahavat Torah Congregation, on different topics about Israel, using guidelines from the Shalom Hartman Institute, entitled, "Engage: Israel's Milestones and Their Meanings."

CHAPTER FOUR

"Mary Fisher's speech was later ranked…"
Found in "The Top 100 Speeches of the 20th Century by Rank," American Rhetoric, compiled by Michael Eidenmuller.

"How Hesed and Gevurah occur in daily life…"
Described in detail in Chapter Three of the book "More Fully Alive: The Benefits of Using Jewish Wisdom for Responding to Stress and Overload, by Leonard Felder, (Los Angeles: JFuture Books, 2016).

"The airline industry said…"
See Allan Brandt, "The Cigarette Century," (New York: Basic Books, 2007), pp. 303-4.

"The chairman of the Civil Aeronautics Board sided with…."
See "CAB Flip-flops on Smoking Policy," Washington Post, June 1, 1984, p. 10.

"Senator Jesse Helms tried to stop the bill…"
See John Cushman, "Senate Weighs Ban on Flight Smoking," New York Times, September 14, 1989.

"Secretary of Transportation Elizabeth Dole insisted…"
See Douglas Jehl, "Senate Acts to Ban Smoking on 70% of Airline Flights," Los Angeles Times, October 30, 1987.

"Senator Lautenberg and a young House member named Dick Durbin…"
See Glenn Kramon, "Smoking Ban Near on Flights in U.S.," New York Times, April 17, 1988.

"The Republicans and the chemical industry tried to block…"
See Lynn Bergeson and Charles Auer, "Toxic Substances Control Act," American Bar Association, Section Newsletters, October 4, 2018.

"According to Fred Krupp on cooperation…."
See Fred Krupp, "This Story of Bipartisanship Will Make You Believe in Government Again," HuffPost, July 13, 2016.

CHAPTER FIVE

"In Leviticus 18…" This chapter will explore several different ways of interpreting Leviticus 18:22.

"We don't just settle for the p'shat surface level…"
See Avigdor Bonchek, "Studying the Torah: A Guide to In-depth Interpretation," (Northvale, NJ: Jason Aronson, 1996).

"Numerous scholars view Leviticus 18:22 as possibly being about certain idol-worshiping activities and non-consensual sex…"
See Rabbi Rachel Barenblat, "The Velveteen Rabbi: Re-reading Leviticus 18:22," weblog, May 17, 2004; or Jay Sklar, "The Prohibition Against Homosexual Sex in Leviticus 18:22 and 20:13: Are They Relevant Today?," in Bulletin for Biblical Research, Vol. 28, no. 2 (2018), pp. 165-198; or Jay Michaelson, "God vs. Gay?," (Boston: Beacon Press, 2011), pp. 63-6; or Merissa Nathan Gerson, "What the Talmud Can Teach Us About Sex and Consent," Tablet Magazine, October 3, 2018; or Eve Levavi Feinstein, "The Torah: A Historical and Contextual Approach," TheTorah.com; or Beatrice Brooks, "Fertility Cult Functionaries in the Old Testament," Journal of Biblical Literature, Vol. 60, no. 3 (September 1941), pp. 227-253; or Cyrus Gordon, "Middle Eastern Religious Practices and Institutions," www.britannica.com, Encyclopedia Brittanica.

"The Torah urges not to mistreat the servant…"
See Exodus 21:7-11, Leviticus 25:39-43, Leviticus 25:45-56, Deuteronomy 15:12-15, Deuteronomy 23:15, and Martin Goodman, "Rome and Jerusalem: The Clash of Ancient Civilizations," (New York: Penguin, 2007).

"The American Psychiatric Association ruled in the early 1970's…"
See "The APA Ruling on Homosexuality," New York Times, December 23, 1973, or Neel Burton, "When Homosexuality Stopped Being a Mental Disorder," Psychology Today, September 18, 2015.

"Rabbi Jonathan Sacks has written that…"
See the Introduction by Rabbi Sacks to "Judaism and Homosexuality: An Authentic Orthodox View" by Rabbi Chaim Rapoport, 2004.

"Rabbi Daniel Landes wrote…"
See Rabbi Landes, "We Need Gay Orthodox Rabbis," Jewish Journal, May 28, 2019.

"Rabbi Joseph Dweck taught on the premise…"
See "Rabbi Dweck Can Remain as Sephardic Leader, Rabbinic Panel Says," The Jewish Chronicle, July 19, 2017.

"Rabbi Yosef Kanefsky has written…"
See Rabbi Kanefsky, "An Orthodox Gay Wedding?," in Morethodoxy: Exploring the Breadth, Depth and Passion of Orthodox Judaism, November 18, 2011; or Rabbi Yosef Kanefsky, "A More Modern View of Homosexuality," Jewish Journal, December 5, 2012.

"Rabbi Shmuly Yanklowitz has written…"
See Rabbi Yanklowitz, "5 Reasons Being an Orthodox Rabbi Compelled Me to Support Gay Marriage," The Huffington Post, December 19, 2013.

"Chief Rabbi Ephraim Mirvis wrote…"
See "The Well-being of LGBT+ Pupils: A Guide for Orthodox Jewish Schools," at Keshetuk.org; or Esther Kustanowitz, "UK Guide Offers Safe Space to Orthodox LGBT+ Students," Jewish Journal, May 31, 2019.

"Rabbi Elliot Dorff cited…"
See John Dart, "Conservative Judaism Re-Examines Views on Gays and Lesbians," Los Angeles Times, July 25, 1992; or Rabbi Elliot Dorff, "Homosexuality, Choice, and Jewish Law," in "Matters of Life and Death: A Jewish Approach to Modern Medical Ethics," (Jewish Publication Society, 2003).

"Rabbi Bradley Shavit Artson argued that…"
See "Homosexuality and Judaism: A New Response for a New Reality," Academia.edu, 1992; "Gays and Lesbians: An Innovative Legal Position," Jewish Spectator, Winter 1990-91; and "Homosexuality and Judaism: Synthesis or Impasse," New Menorah, Spring 1991.

"Like Hillel and Shammai…"
See Marcus Jastrow, "Bet Hillel and Bet Shammai" in JewishEncyclopedia. com.

"Rabbi Heschel and radical amazement…"

See "Abraham Joshua Heschel, "Prayer and Radical Amazement," www.campramahne.org or Rabbi Abraham Joshua Heschel, "Radical Amazement," Awakin.org

"At least six variations of gender can be found…"

See David Meyer, "What the Torah Teaches Us About Gender Flexibility and Transgender Justice," Blog article, September 20, 2018; or Rabbi Elliot Kukla, "Trans Torah," Blog article, sojournsd.org, June 1, 2015; or Charlotte Elisheva Fonrobert, "Gender Identity in Halakhic Discourse," Jewish Women's Archive, JWA.org; or Rabbi Elliot Kukla and Rabbi Reuben Zellman, "Created by the Hand of Heaven: A Jewish Approach to Intersexuality," Keshetonline.org, April 21, 2007.

CHAPTER SIX

"The Amidah prayer begins with the words…"

See B.S. Jacobson, "The Weekday Siddur: An Exposition and Analysis, (Tel Aviv: Sinai, 1978), p. 215, or Macy Nulman, "The Encyclopedia of Jewish Prayer," (Northvale, NJ: Jason Aronson, 1993), p. 59, or Responsa Panim Me'irot, pt. 1, ch. 37.

"Some scholars have suggested the Kaddish…"

See Rabbi Nancy Fuchs-Kreimer, "You Shall Not Lift Up the Name of Adonai Your God for Vain Purpose," in "Broken Tablets," (Woodstock, Vt: Jewish Lights, 1999); or Aviezer Ravitzky, "Rabbi Joseph Soloveitchik on Human Knowledge," Modern Judaism, vol. 6, no. 2, May 1986, pp. 157-88; or Rabbeinu Bahya ibn Paquda, "Chovos Halevavos Shaar Yichud (Duties of the Heart)," chapter 10, English translation by Rabbi Yosef, (Jerusalem: Sebag, 2017).

"As one scholar explained the Kaddish…"

From a Saturday morning teaching by Rabbi Mordecai Finley, Ohr HaTorah Congregation, Los Angeles, 1998.

"Some say the Torah mentions at least 36 times…"

See Rabbi Jonathan Sacks, "Mishpatim—Loving the Stranger," on rabbisacks.org; or Rabbi Eliezer, Babylonian Talmud, Bava M'tzia, 59b; or

Rabbi Reuven Firestone, "The Commandment to Love and Help the Stranger," ReformJudaism.org; or Rachel Farbiarz, "Treatment of the Stranger," MyJewishLearning.com

ACKNOWLEDGMENTS

I am thankful to a wide variety of people who helped this book become a reality. There are too many names to list, but I will mention a few.

At the National Conference of Christians and Jews, Glen Poling, Neil Van Steenbergen, Bernice Van Steenbergen, Robin Siegal, Dennis Hicks, Michael Ellington, Melinda Garcia, Glen Effertz, Crystal Jones, Rita Nakashima Brock, Laura Pawlowski, Lecia Brooks, Marilyn Graves, and many others taught me how to create healthy dialogues between diverse individuals. In addition, Janet Sternfeld Davis and Lucky Lynch taught me how to help people talk about their profound religious differences in a caring and productive way.

At Ahavat Torah Congregation, dozens of men and women have been helpful to me during the 14 years we have been studying together in Rabbi Miriam Hamrell's weekly Mussar discussion group on how to use Jewish teachings for dealing with daily personal and ethical challenges.

For many years in Detroit, New York, Los Angeles, and elsewhere, numerous rabbis have guided me on how to apply Jewish teachings to life's toughest moments. They include Rabbi M. Robert Syme, Rabbi Ted Falcon, Rabbi David Cooper, Rabbi Zalman Schachter Shalomi, Rabbi Laura Geller, Rabbi Debra Orenstein, Rabbi Miriam Hamrell, and many others.

Several friends, colleagues, and family members have opened me up to look at ways to grow and overcome my blind spots, including Teri Bernstein, Catherine Coulson, Marc Sirinsky, Peter and Carol Reiss, Jean Katz, Judith Rivin, Arlene Levin, Nancy Shapiro Pikelny, Catherin Mahlin, Miriam Raviv, Tony Dodge, Coleman and Nadine Colla, Sandra

Kaler, Patricia Amrhein, Julie Madorsky, and my sisters Janice Ruff, Andi Bittker, and Ruthe Wagner.

Every day I am thankful for the love and honest feedback I receive from my wife and best friend Linda Schorin and my daughter and teacher Aloni Schorin, who help me discover what needs to be improved and how to do it as a family.

I am also grateful for the love and support I received from my beloved mom, Helen Rothenberg Felder, my dad Martin Felder, my stepmom Ena Felder, and for the ongoing support and kindness of many members of the Felder family, the Rothenberg family, the Schorin family, and the Wilstein family.

Most of all, I am thankful to the Infinite Creative Presence that guides me and supports me constantly.

CONVERSATION QUESTIONS

A Note to the Reader: Here are some possible discussion questions you can use in a class, an honest family conversation, a book discussion group, a havurah gathering of friends, or a staff in-service training.

Feel free to change any of these questions to suit your needs. My hope is that each question will allow every person to feel welcomed, heard, included, and treated with respect for their diverse experiences and perspectives.

CHAPTER ONE:
What to Do When It Starts to Get Intense

Question One: As a child or recently, when have you felt pressured or criticized because your way of practicing religion was different from certain influential individuals in your family or community?

Question Two: What are the Jewish mindfulness tools that Dr. Felder suggests from Maimonides and others for disagreeing without being disagreeable?

Question Three: Describe a moment when you were able to stand up for your values without alienating or hurting anyone?

CHAPTER TWO:
How Do You Feel About the #MeToo Issues?

Question One: If you were raising a teenage or adult son or daughter, what would you teach them about how to be respectful regarding sexuality and what makes someone feel uncomfortable or harassed?

Question Two: What are the steps Dr. Felder explores (or that you would recommend) for helping the person who was sexually harassed or put in an uncomfortable situation?

Question Three: What are the teshuvah steps described in Chapter Two (or that you would recommend) for the person who was sexually manipulative or caused someone to feel uncomfortable?

CHAPTER THREE:
What Gets on Your Nerves When People Talk About Israel

Question One: In the past several years, when have you felt upset about the way people were commenting about Israeli policies or Middle East controversies?

Question Two: When have you been able to honor both the perspective of the descendants of Hagar and the descendants of Sarah?

Question Three: What are the steps that Dr. Felder recommends (or that you would recommend) for discussing Israel in a public setting without attacking one another or shunning those who have differing viewpoints?

CHAPTER FOUR:
Are There Red vs. Blue Tensions in Your Life Lately?

Question One: What has been happening politically in your family, your workplace, your school, or your friendships lately that has resulted in hurt feelings or harsh words?

Question Two: Using the suggestions from Chapter Four, what is a strength, a good quality, or a positive habit you see in the person whose political views are quite different from your own?

Question Three: What is an example of when you have built a bridge or some teamwork with someone who differs from you politically and it resulted in something constructive?

CHAPTER FIVE:
What's Your Personal Journey Regarding LGBT Struggles

Question One: Prior to reading Chapter Five of "We See It So Differently," what did you think was the 'Jewish position' about LGBT inclusiveness? What did you learn or discover from reading how the Orthodox, Conservative, Reform, Reconstructionist, and Renewal movements have wrestled with these issues in recent decades?

Question Two: What would you like to see happen for an LGBT individual at work, at school, in your family, or in your community who might need extra support for how they have been excluded or talked about in less-than-respectful ways?

Question Three: What are the steps from Chapter Five that might help someone you know who is uncomfortable or somewhat opposed regarding LGBT issues and might need more time or conversations in order to become a possible ally?

CHAPTER SIX:
What Happens When You Disagree About Religious Decisions and Holiday Gatherings

Question One: In what ways are you someone who practices religion and holidays because of "tradition" and "commandments," and in what ways are you someone who practices religion and holidays because of "how they inspire you" and "how they feel personally meaningful."

Question Two: What have you done in previous years (or you could do in the future) to make Jewish holiday and Shabbat gatherings more enjoyable and engaging for all of your diverse guests?

Question Three: What do you think might help a family member or friend who feels especially cut off from religion to re-connect with the deeper meaning and beauty of an upcoming holiday or special event?

ABOUT THE AUTHOR

Leonard Felder, PhD, is a licensed psychologist in West Los Angeles. He has written fifteen books on Jewish spirituality and personal growth that have sold more than one million copies and have been translated into fourteen languages. These titles include *The Ten Challenges, More Fully Alive, Here I Am, Seven Prayers That Can Change Your Life, Fitting In Is Overrated, The Dilemma of the 21ˢᵗ Century Male,* and *When Difficult Relatives Happen to Good People.* Several of his books have received non-fiction writing awards.

He has been invited to lead discussions on the connection between Jewish texts and daily psychological dilemmas at forty temples and synagogues, fourteen Jewish book fairs, plus dozens of churches and interfaith events nationwide. He has also appeared on more than two hundred radio and television programs, including *The Today Show on NBC, Oprah Winfrey, CNN, The CBS Early Show, NBC Nightly News, National Public Radio, Canada AM,* and *BBC London.*

Active in several volunteer organizations, Dr. Felder received the Distinguished Merit Citation of the National Conference of Christians and Jews for helping to develop innovative programs to combat racism, sexism, homophobia, and religious prejudice.

Originally from Detroit, Michigan, he graduated with high honors from Kenyon College in Ohio and worked in New York as the director of research for Doubleday and Company before completing his PhD in Psychology and becoming a therapist in California. He and his wife Linda Schorin, a visual artist, are the active parents of Aloni Schorin, a young adult with special needs who makes videos and films about Autism, diversity, and inclusion.